THE SMART APPROACH TO
KIDS' ROOMS

CRE▲TIVE
HOMEOWNER®

THE SMART APPROACH TO
KIDS'
ROOMS

Megan Connelly

CREATIVE HOMEOWNER®, Upper Saddle River, New Jersey

Editorial Director: Timothy O. Bakke
Art Director: W. David Houser

Senior Decorating Editor: Kathie Robitz
Decorating Editor: Carolyn Anderson-Feighner
Photo Researcher: Amla Sanghvi
Editorial Assistant: Laura De Ferrari
Proofreaders: Doria Gambino, Stanley Sudol
Indexer: Joanne M. Still

Interior Design Consultant: Michelle Rohrer

Interior Book Design: Monduane Harris
Illustrations: pp. 29, 154–158, Vincent Alessi; pp. 12, 14, 15, 34, 38, 65, 78, 88, 102, 104, 115, 118, 119, 135, 136, 161, 166, Janet Kroenke; all other illustrations, Ian Warpole

Cover Design: Monduane Harris
Cover Photography: Mark Samu
Back Cover Photography (clockwise from top left):
Brian Vanden Brink, Jessie Walker, Mark Samu

Current Printing (last digit)
10 9 8 7 6 5 4 3

The Smart Approach to Kids' Rooms, First Edition
Library of Congress Catalog Card Number: 00-101554
ISBN: 1-58011-027-4

CREATIVE HOMEOWNER®
A Division of Federal Marketing Corp.
24 Park Way
Upper Saddle River, NJ 07458
Web site: **www.creativehomeowner.com**

DEDICATION

For my beautiful children, Sheila and Aedan, and their wonderful father, Joe.

ACKNOWLEDGMENTS

The completion of this book would hardly have been possible without the encouragement, support, and patience of my editor, Kathie Robitz. In this, as in all things, she is one of a kind. My appreciation also extends to Creative Homeowner for believing in this project.

In addition, I would like to thank the following resources: The Juvenile Products Manufacturers Association, The Consumer Product Safety Commission, The Allergy and Asthma Network of Fairfax, Virginia, and the countless parents of children with special needs who have taken to the Internet to share their experiences and innovative ideas for enhancing the lives of their children.

CONTENTS

Introduction

Bending over to tuck the blanket into the crib, your excitement builds as you finish putting the last few touches in the nursery you have decorated for your first bundle of joy. Along with your anticipation, you hope that everything is safe, secure, and just right for the baby to be. As you glance around the room, you might ask yourself if you should have chosen the soothing pastel colors instead of the stimulating primaries. Don't worry; someday that tiny child will have no trouble telling you exactly what she likes. The colors you choose now might someday seem too childish to someone who is trying to state her independence.

Children grow up too fast. Just when you become comfortable with one phase, they mature and their tastes—and requirements—change. No problem. *The Smart Approach to Kids' Rooms* can help you. It will show you how to work with space, choose the right colors, and shop for furniture, flooring, and window treatments while sticking to a budget. Looking for creative ideas and projects you can do yourself? Easy-to-follow instructions show you how to add personality to the room with paint, paper, and fabric crafts. If your child has special needs, *The Smart Approach to Kids' Rooms* has advice for creating an accessible, healthy, yet attractive environment.

When you're ready to start, sit down with your child and read this book together. You may be inspired by what others have done—and, hopefully, you will both come up with great ideas of your own.

More than a place to sleep, your child's room should be the kind of personal setting that will inspire creativity, individuality, and healthy play.

CHAPTER 1

In The Beginning

At first, it seems as though everyone lives in the baby's room. Life centers on the needs of the newest member of the family. But as time goes on, a child's room becomes a place apart from the other family spaces. It takes on the parents' wishes for the child and the child's own character. That's why decorating the room can be fun. For the parents of very young children, the project is a chance to re-create some of their own childhood fantasies. As children grow and begin to develop preferences, Mom, Dad, and the kids can make decisions about furniture, colors, patterns, and themes together. Whatever the case, don't order the new carpeting or run off to the paint store yet. For the best result, one that pleases parents and child alike, it pays to plan. Whether the decorating scheme will be classic or totally unique and new, the goal is to create a balanced room that is both stimulating and soothing. To do it right, know ahead of time how much work will be entailed and what you will have to spend on the project. While you're doing your planning, remember that this is the one room in the house that is strictly your child's. He will do a lot of things in there besides sleeping: playing, alone or with friends; listening to music; reading; studying; and keeping up with hobbies. Try to accommodate all of these functions while making the room an attractive and comfortable haven that suits your child's individuality. That way you won't have to redecorate for years to come.

There are few basics that are necessary in a nursery aside from the crib. As a child grows, each new age will bring a new set of needs for the room.

SHOULD YOU DO IT YOURSELF?

Answer these questions honestly. Then judge for yourself.

▶ How extensive is the project? If you're just giving the room a face-lift, you can probably handle the job. If something requires special skill, such as electrical work or building bookshelves, leave it to a professional.

▶ Do you have enough spare time to commit to the project? Painting the walls may take a weekend; redesigning the floor plan, shopping, and ordering furniture can take weeks.

▶ Are you patient and persistent? Can you follow through to the end? Don't start anything you can't finish.

▶ Do you enjoy physical work, such as removing and hanging wallpaper, installing flooring material, or refinishing furniture?

▶ Have you ever done any of this kind of work before?

▶ Do you know what tools are required for specific jobs? Do you have them?

▶ Will you need assistance? If a task requires more than two hands, can you can get the help you need when you need it?

▶ Do you have the confidence to make all of the decorating decisions yourself? If you hit a snag, are you willing to call in a consultant, such as professional interior designer? Is there any room in your budget to cover the cost of bringing in a professional if you make a mistake you can't fix yourself?

In this chapter, you'll learn how to develop a plan of action, which will begin with taking a critical look at the existing space, and trying various ways, on paper, for making improvements. Follow the easy steps that are on pages 14 and 15 to help with the process. After you've made your analysis, you'll be able to organize a list of objectives — things you want to achieve with the new design—and decide whom you want to do the work. (If you plan to do all of the work yourself, take the quiz on the left to see if this is a realistic idea.)

This nursery décor strikes the right balance. Replace the crib with a bed and the room will serve well for years.

It's always smart to put together a realistic budget for a project ahead of time so that you don't get caught short midway through the renovation project. If you're all thumbs when it comes to hammering out figures, follow the advice that begins on page 22.

Evaluating the Space

More than anything else, you can rely on your own personal taste and intuition, and that of your child's, to design the room because there are no hard and fast rules for decorating. But it always helps to keep in mind the basic principles of scale,

DESIGN BASICS. Professionals rely on the principles of scale and proportion, line, balance, harmony, and rhythm when designing a room. By applying these concepts you'll be able to make the most of the room's best attributes, and play down the less-appealing features of the space.

▶ *Scale and proportion* work hand in hand. Scale refers to the size of something as it relates to the size of everything else. Proportion refers to the relationship of objects to one another based on size.

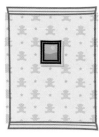

▶ *Line* defines and shapes space. Vertical lines appear strong; horizontal lines appear restful; diagonal lines express motion or transition; curved lines denote softness.

▶ *Balance* refers to the even placement of things of varying sizes and shapes around the room. Balanced relationships can be either symmetrical or asymmetrical.

▶ *Harmony* is achieved when everything coordinates within one scheme or motif.

▶ *Rhythm* refers to repeated forms. While harmony pulls a room together, rhythm, or repetition of a pattern or shape, moves your eye around it.

proportion, line, balance, harmony, and rhythm when examining space — and all of the ways to fill it up. This is what professional designers do to create interiors that are both pleasing to the eye and practical for living. To get acquainted with these concepts, consult the Smart Tip box, "Design Basics" on the previous page.

It's an excellent idea to put your thoughts on paper. So, with a notepad and pencil in hand, take a walk around the room at various times of the day. Jot down everything you like and don't like about the room. Is it too small or too large? Is it oddly shaped? Are the furnishings the proper scale for the space? Is it easy or difficult to arrange furniture in the room? How many doors and windows are there? Are they conveniently placed? Is the room too dark or too bright at certain times of the day? Are there enough closets and other types of storage space? You may have to live with some or all of the physical drawbacks of the space, but recognizing them will inspire you to find ways around them.

Next, look at the condition of the surfaces. Do the walls simply need re-painting or new wallpaper, or is there damage that requires repair? Kids can be pretty tough on floors and carpeting. Take stock of the existing furniture. Is it adequate for your child's needs? What condition is it in? Minor damage to the finish, missing knobs, drawers that stick or need re-gluing are easy repair jobs. Don't forget to get input from the person who occupies the room, too. Her perception of the space is the most important aspect of your analysis.

Your notes can be brief, but make them thorough. This will help you to focus on what existing features can stay and what needs to be changed. Here's how to look at the space critically and organize your thoughts into action.

 ONE: **Measure up.** Take the overall dimensions of the room using a steel measuring tape; include the size of all of the openings (doors and windows). If there are any fixed features, such as a built-in desk or bookcases, measure and record their sizes, too.

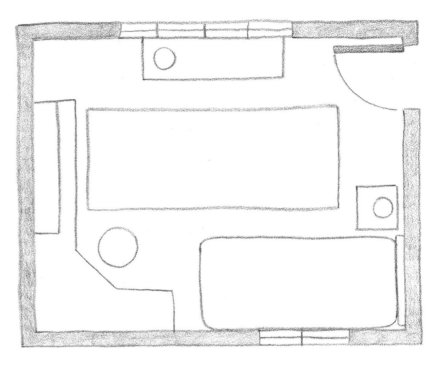

Take careful measurements, and then draw a freehand sketch of the space. Be sure to note the electrical outlets, cable and phone jacks, and any permanent features such as a closet or built-in bookcase.

Measure the existing furniture. With just a few adjustments to the layout, you may save yourself the expense of buying something new. If you're planning shelf storage for large toys, a TV, stereo, and computer equipment, measure them.

Make a freehand sketch of the space and the furnishings, and list the measurements you've taken in the margin. Don't forget to note the electrical switches and outlets, cable and phone jacks, radiators, heat registers, air ducts, and light fixtures.

TWO: **Draw a floor plan to scale.** You'll find this invaluable as a reference when you're shopping for furniture or arranging the layout of the room. Consult the Appendix, which shows the standard symbols used to indicate permanent features on your plan. Use shorthand; for 3 feet and 2 inches write 3' 2" and so on.

Work on $1/4$-inch graph paper. Each square will represent one foot. For example, if a wall measures 15 feet, the line you draw to indicate that wall will use 15 squares. Use a ruler or straightedge to make your lines; then record your measurements.

Draw a floor plan to scale. On paper, try out different furniture arrangements, and then take the drawing with you when you shop.

To try out different furniture arrangements, first draw and cut out furniture templates, using the same 1/4-inch scale. Refer to the standard furniture symbols in the Appendix. Each one is drawn to scale based on average dimensions, but you'll have to adjust the scale to your furniture's true size. If you plan to buy new pieces, ask the salesperson to give you the manufacturer's spec sheets, which will include dimensions. Never guess about size.

THREE: **Create a focal point.** When you're playing with the room's layout and furniture arrangement, start by placing the largest piece first; that's typically the bed — the room's focal point. The focal point is the one element that grabs your attention when first you walk into the room. Even if it's a simple twin-size bed, where you locate it and how you dress it makes an impact on the overall look of the room.

By working out the details on paper, the designer made the most of the space. Built-in storage, left, became part of the plan, and an elaborate game-board motif, above, was painted on the floor.

Clearances. Whenever possible, plan enough space around the furniture to use it comfortably. For example, if there will be under-bed storage, such as roll-out drawers, make sure there's enough room on the side of the bed to pull the drawers out. Although you're limited by the actual size of the room, professionals recommend the following minimum allowances, whenever possible:

✳ 22 inches of space around the bed

✳ 36 inches of space between the bed and any door that opens into the room

✳ 18 inches between two beds that are placed side by side to accommodate a small night table and a pathway

A queen-size mattress was situated on a low platform, above left, to safely ease the transition from crib to grown-up bed. Drawers built into the platform, above, do not obstruct traffic.

✳ 3 feet of space in front of a closet for dressing and sorting items of clothing

✳ 40 inches of space into the room to open dresser drawers

✳ 10 to 20 inches of space to sit comfortably in a chair at a desk, plus 12 to 16 more inches to pull back the chair and rise from it

✳ a distance that is three times the size of the TV screen for optimum viewing

Take note of the location of vents, heating or air-conditioning units, phone jacks, and electrical switches and outlets. Maintain a distance of 6 inches between baseboard heating and air-conditioning units and furniture. Don't block or obstruct outlets or switches.

Traffic Patterns. Make them as convenient as possible for you and your children. For example, in a nursery, locate the changing table closest to the door and the crib farther into the room.

Traffic patterns are especially important in shared rooms. Allow clearances for one child to pass another child without disruption when someone is seated at a desk or play area. Strategic storage in the play area will be used more often than something

that's inconvenient. If your kids play in the middle of the floor, a rolling cart that can be pushed against the wall when not in use can make picking up toys easier.

Adaptability. Floor plans that detail present and future needs can help when you're making decisions about furniture. If you're planning to stay in the same house, consider how the room you design now can be adapted later as your child grows older and requires more furniture and storage.

Twin beds fit snugly at one end of this room, below left, but there is enough space between them for easy access. A chest, below, at the foot of each bed provides storage. The room's occupants share the table-and-chair set, bottom right.

Shared Spaces

Common areas and equally important private ones are necessary to preserve the peace in a room shared by two children. Size isn't as important as organized function paired with an understanding of the two unique personalities and needs of the two kids who will use the room.

When those two children are very young, a shared play area can totally dominate the space. That means you'll have to find a way to partially block off the sleeping area so that one child can rest quietly while the other plays, if necessary. Doubled storage space for toys helps to promote shared responsibility. Each child should be expected to care for his own things.

School-age kids require separate quiet places for reading, studying, and hobby pursuits. Take into account the different study habits and interests of siblings when you're planning these places. As a child differentiates herself and develops her own interests, her needs for reserved space, where she is totally in control, becomes more important for maturing with a healthy sense of self. Both children benefit from having clearly defined areas where the other child cannot play or use things without asking her roommate first.

The problems are somewhat more difficult when children who are separated by several years share space. Younger children don't understand property rights as yet. In these situations, walls or half-walls make sharing a room easier.

DIVIDING UP THE SPACE

Begin by listing the needs of each child. In most cases, kids can share some areas. Play space, TV viewing, and hobby tables are often accommodating to overlapping needs. For older children, desks and computer equipment may have to be planned separately for each child. Something such as an aquarium or a special wall decoration should be equally available to both children, unless there is agreement by both children and parents to the contrary.

Before you divide up the space in a room, involve the children in the planning process. Who gets what should be decided up front; that way everybody will be happy with the results.

MORE IDEAS FOR SHARED ROOMS. Even when you can't physically divide a room, you can use a few visual tricks that will make both kids feel like they've got their own private space.

▶ Position the heads of the beds so that the children are looking away from each other, not toward each another.

▶ Locate reading or task lighting so that it's confined to each child's area without spillover.

▶ Use a different color to identify each child's belongings. Use a common print or a third color to bridge the two. (See Chapter 2, "Introducing Color, Pattern, & Texture," page 24, for more tips.)

▶ If both kids like the same color, go into reverse. For example, use white polka dots on a blue background for one child's bedding, and then use blue polka dots on a white background for the other one. Many fabrics are available in reverse colorations.

▶ If one section of the room is cut off from natural light and there's no outside wall where you can add another window, consider a roof window or skylight to brighten the darker half of the space.

▶ Use mirrors to make small areas appear larger.

Furniture Dividers. Modular furniture that incorporates units for sleeping, studying, and storage can be used effectively to divide space in a shared room. (See "Modular Systems," on page 44 in Chapter 3, "Furnishings For Your Child's Room.") It allows for design flexibility in almost any layout.

Tall freestanding bookcases are another good idea for divvying up space in a room. Enclosed units can be used back to back or side by side. In the latter case, the backs can provide a surface for posters, or your children can use them as bulletin boards. If this arrangement blocks the light, consider half-size bookcases or freestanding open shelving. Hang a fabric shade from the top of an open shelving unit. When privacy is desired, the shade can be rolled down.

Armoires and wardrobes are another solution. Place them back to back or stagger them to create a room divider. For added safety with any freestanding furniture, anchor it to the floor or ceiling, using L-brackets.

Half Walls. A good way to delineate space is with a half wall. If your budget allows, hire a carpenter to construct one at wainscot level, 30 to 40 inches high. Half walls provide privacy for children while they're seated or lying in bed, and at the same time allow good light and air circulation throughout both sides of the room. Plus, you can build storage into the divider.

MODIFYING THE SHAPE OF A ROOM

Some rooms are just oddly shaped. But you can disguise this imperfection, or draw attention away from it, with visual tricks. For example, if the room is

* *Long,* divide the space by creating two separate, major groupings of furniture. One way is to make a sleeping space apart from the play and work zone. Use area rugs to anchor each group in the divided space. You can also use square shapes, such as a square area rug, to "widen" the space.

* *Narrow,* arrange furniture on the diagonal. Place the bed catty-cornered. Again, introduce more squares into the room — cube-shaped chests or a large square-shape mirror, for example. Group art in a square-shape arrangement on a major wall.

* *Low,* add height with tall furnishings, such as tall bookcases, a highboy dresser, or an armoire. You might also consider window treatments that extend above the window frame and hang from the area just below the ceiling to the floor. Use as many vertical lines in the room as possible, even on wall and fabric treatments. Vertical stripe wallpaper or curtains are good examples.

* *Tall,* lower the scale of the space by incorporating more horizontal lines in the room. Install molding half or three quarters of the way up the walls to visually shorten them. Hang pictures lower on the wall.

A dramatic window treatment, right, is also practical in this large nursery with a vaulted ceiling. Its curvaceous swags soften the angles of the room; its height is in good proportion to the volume of the space.

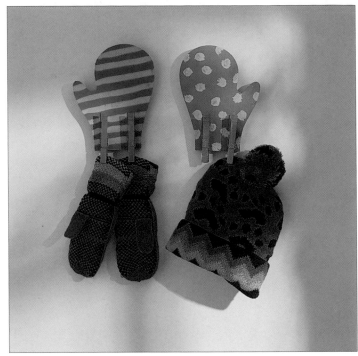

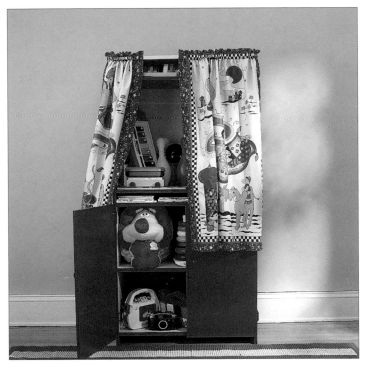

Putting things away can be fun. Here are lots of colorful, playful solutions for keeping kids' stuff neat and off the floor. Clockwise, from the top left, the creative ideas utilize simple cabinets, clothespins, chests, plastic crates, stacked plastic boxes with sliding drawers, fabric bags, and curtain closures.

Sometimes rooms, particularly those built under attic eaves, have too many angles, which makes the space look chopped up. An easy way to camouflage this problem is by painting all of the surfaces, including the ceiling, one color. Wallpaper that has a mini print will accomplish the same thing.

MORE STRATEGIES FOR SUCCESS

Decorating most kids' rooms puts you up against one of the most common problems most parents face: lack of space. To complicate matters, kids have a lot of stuff, and they're pack rats. They will collect everything from stuffed animals to computer software (not to mention the plastic trinkets that come with fast-food meals) and an assortment of other paraphernalia that finds its way into the room, and never comes out. But before you attempt to provide a place for everything, remember: Everything will seldom be kept in its designated place, and more of it is always on the way.

You can avoid a lot of the conflict that inevitably develops over messy rooms by setting aside a day — once a week, once a month, or at the beginning of each season, whatever suits you — to do an inventory, with your child, of what stays and what goes. Begin with the clothes. If it no longer fits or hasn't been worn in a while, get rid of it. Give it to charity, hand it down, or toss it — just get it out of the room.

Next, hit the toys. Whatever lies untouched for a while, quietly pack off to the attic or basement. When the present favorites lose their appeal, stow them away, and then bring out the ones in storage. This rotation keeps clutter down. New toys simply replace current ones, which can be packed away with the others. Keep this process ongoing. School-age kids might balk, but reassure them by letting them know that they may exchange any stored item for something that's in their room. Admittedly, the older the child , the harder it is to enforce this system. But it's worth a try. Sometimes you have to remind yourself that most kids' rooms are cluttered, so live with it.

A SAMPLE BUDGET WORKSHEET

Item	Manufacturer/ Retailer	Style/ Pattern	Color	Immediate Purchase Costs	Future Purchase Costs
Furniture:					
Bed	Slocum's	Sleigh Bed	White	500	
Mattress set	Slocum's	#0335	—	350	
Armoire	Slocum's	#080	Unfinished		800
Old Dresser Paint	Noname	Premium	White	30	
Wall Treatments:					
Paint	Noname	Premium	Pink Cheeks	60	
Wallpaper	Ashford's	Dance Class	Rose		250
Window Treatments:					
Blinds	WindowWorld	Plain Mini	White	50	
Curtains	WindowWorld	Candy Stripe	Pink		100
Valance	WindowWorld	Candy Stripe	Pink	30	
Floorings:					
Wall-to-Wall Carpeting	Carpet City	Blush	Lt. Beige		500
Area Rug	Slocum's	Posies	Pastels	50	
Lighting:					
Lamps	Slocum's	Candlestick	White	100	
Bedding:					
Quilt	Slocum's	Dancing Bears	Lavender	50	
Sham	Slocum's	Dancing Bears	Lavender	20	
Sheet set	Slocum's	Plain Percale	White	25	
Accessories:					
Wall art	The Boutique	Hearts & Flowers	—	75	
Mirror	The Boutique	Wicker	White	25	
Bulletin Board	Toy Shop	—	—	10	
			TOTALS	**$1,375**	**$1,650**

Make a budget worksheet listing all the elements of the project. Attach any sample photos that you have saved from magazines that show the ideas or the look you want to achieve.

School worksheets, tests, and artwork can quickly turn a room into a real mess if there's no place to organize them. A small metal file cabinet is inexpensive, and it doesn't take up much space. You can spray-paint it to go with the décor, or simply cover it up with a pretty tablecloth and let it double as a nightstand. Make a large hanging file for papers from each grade. Oversized artwork can be stored in a flat art portfolio that can slip easily into a closet for safekeeping.

Even the smallest room can store things efficiently if you make the most out of every square inch. Closet and drawer organizing systems are worthwhile investments. Plastic stacking bins, under-bed drawers and boxes, and shelving all help to keep stuff out of sight without much effort or added expenditure.

Developing a Budget

Before getting carried away with plans or ideas, devise a budget for the project. You may already know your bottom line: the total amount you can afford to spend. With that in mind, make a list of everything you'd like to buy for the room. Something you can't afford now may be a realistic purchase six months from now. You don't have to make all of your changes right away. Take your shopping list with you, and make product and price comparisons. Note all of the style and item numbers, as well as the names of the colors and patterns; you'll need that information, especially for things you may put off purchasing until later. When you've narrowed down your selections, create a worksheet, such as the one on the opposite page. It will show you where you stand, and it can be a permanent record for your files.

PROFESSIONAL FEES

What if you have to bring in professional help? Sometimes the most practical thing you can do to keep costs down is to seek professional help. Whether it's for a design consultation or for the services of a contractor, it often makes more sense to pay for someone's expertise rather than risk costly mistakes. Most professionals will gladly give you an estimate. Take that figure and pad it a bit — just to be on the safe side. You never know what problem may come up that can boost the original estimated costs of the job. Expect to pay more and you *might* come out ahead.

Interior Designers. The practiced eye of a professional designer can rearrange or reuse many of the things you already own. By offering suggestions for how you can refinish or relocate a piece of furniture, or where you can find great buys on secondhand stuff, he can save you lots of money in the long run. Even little tips about arranging wall art, eliminating clutter, using color effectively, or coordinating prints and fabrics are worth the relatively few dollars you'll spend for the advice. Many interior designers will consult for an hourly rate, which can be less than $100 in some cases. Larger projects are often negotiated for a flat fee. Don't be afraid to ask for design advice where you shop; sometimes, it's free.

Contractors. Tradespeople such as carpenters, painters, and wallpaper hangers typically work for an hourly rate. That rate varies across the country. On the East Coast, it's higher than in the Midwest, for example. When a contractor gives you an estimate, it's a compilation of how much time she thinks it will take to do the work, plus the cost of materials, such as paint. Get a few estimates (and at least three references) before hiring someone to do any work for you.

Bright primary colors were used as accents in this easily adaptable all-white room. When it is time to make a change, new curtains and different-color accent pieces will do it.

Introducing Color, Pattern, & Texture

$\mathcal{K}$ids have definite opinions about color—opinions that may be very different from your own. Choosing a color scheme for a nursery may be entirely up to you, but by the time your son or daughter reaches the toddler stage, he or she will already show preferences for particular colors. Usually by mid-elementary school age, she will want to help decide on the scheme for her room. And you can count on your preteen or teenage child to insist on a color palette that expresses her individuality.

Experts say that babies distinguish shapes and contrast most clearly, as opposed to different colors. Perhaps, black-and-white contrasts are more interesting to a newborn, who may miss the nuances of subtle contrasts until his eyes develop more fully, but it won't be long until he can distinguish sharply defined, bright colors.

If you've planned a soft pastel palette for your baby's room, don't worry. These theories don't have to determine the color scheme of the entire room; you can add bright colors and contrasts to a nursery through toys, linens, or accessories. In fact, some older babies may need the calming effect of soft colors rather than the sight stimulation of bold, primary hues. The bottom line is: Use the colors you like best in the nursery without worry. For the most part, the only things that matter to your baby is sleep and the next feeding.

Exotic-looking furniture and a wildly extravagant wall-and-ceiling mural elicit flights of fancy in this child's room. The adventuresome mixture incorporates many colors, patterns, and textures in its bold design.

Four different color schemes on these pages, ranging from vibrant orange to cool green, luminous yellows, and soft pink, evoke various moods. Depending on the age of your child, let her specify a preference.

If your child is older but not quite old enough to choose a favorite color, there are ways to determine likes and dislikes, mostly by observation. For example, look over your child's drawings. Is there a dominant color that you see repeatedly? Examine her wardrobe. Most kids choose clothes based on color preference. Make a game of it. Sit down with your child and ask her to pick out her favorite colored blocks and organize them by preference. You can do this with crayons, markers, paints, toys, or any other multicolored resource around the house. Sometimes a special object, such as a much-loved blanket or quilt, a poster or framed print, a cartoon character, or a favorite stuffed animal, can inspire an idea for a color accent or even an entire room's color scheme.

Exuberant red and green accents add vitality to an otherwise all-white room.

surface in the room, at least in linens, in accessories, or on walls that can easily be repainted later. Plain white walls may seem unimaginative and boring, perhaps. But neutral surfaces allow you to introduce an unlimited number of colors and patterns in other ways. Plus, there's the advantage of being able to change the entire look of a room by simply hanging new curtains or changing to another color bedspread or quilt. All-white walls also let your trend-conscious youngster introduce a few faddish colors or prints to the room that can be discarded inexpensively when something new comes along.

One of the smartest things you can do before committing to a color scheme is to learn how to use color effectively.

How Color Works

Light reflected through a prism creates a rainbow, known as the color spectrum. Each band of color blends into the next, from red to ultraviolet. The longest band is red, then orange, yellow, green, blue, violet. Modern color theory takes those bands from the spectrum and forms them into a circle called the color wheel in order to show the relationship of one color to another.

The color wheel includes primary colors (red, blue, yellow), secondary colors (green, orange, violet), and tertiary colors (red-blue, blue-red, for example). Secondary colors are made by mixing two primaries, such as blue and yellow to make green. A primary color and a secondary color are mixed to make tertiary colors, such as blue and green to make turquoise.

By the time most children are three or four years old, they have developed definite color preferences. Typically, they'll gravitate toward bright hues. (Not every little girl favors pink and purple.) Their tastes start to become more sophisticated as they enter their adolescent and teen years.

Should you insist that the colors chosen by your kids for their rooms coordinate with the scheme you've selected for the rest of the house? That's entirely up to you. But even the most outlandish color preferences can be expressed, if not on every

Colors vary in their intensity — that is, the level of the color's purity or saturation. The primaries, secondaries, and tertiaries represent colors at their full intensity. There are several ways to lessen a color's intensity. You can lighten it with white to form a tint, darken it with black to create a shade, or add gray to arrive at a tone. In addition to changing the intensity of a color, these methods affect what is known as the color's value. *Value* is the lightness or darkness of a color. Tinting gives a color a lighter value; shading makes it a darker value. A *hue* is simply another term for color.

PUTTING THE COLOR WHEEL TO WORK FOR YOU

Color schemes are developed by combining colors, using their relationship to one another on the color wheel as a guide. Once you've decided on a basic or main color, you can develop an outstanding scheme around it. Use the color wheel to help you envision certain color combinations for your child's room.

Monochromatic Schemes. These are the easiest to develop because they use just one color; examples include totally pink rooms or totally blue rooms. You can use the color in various intensities and with different textures and patterns to create interest. To freshen the look of a monochromatic scheme over the years, all you have to do is change the accent colors. Introduce new colors with accessories or new curtains, for example.

Analogous Schemes. These are invariably pleasing, as well as easy to develop, because they use colors that are next to one another on the color wheel. An example is pink (technically, red tinted with white) and purple (actually, violet-red) a popular combination with young girls. Another combination, one that is often favored for boys, is blue and green-blue. You can play with variations in value, intensity, and texture to add interest to these color schemes.

Color Wheel Combinations

The color wheel is a useful tool for pairing colors. Basically, it presents the spectrum of hues as a circle. The primary colors (yellow, blue, and red) are combined in the remaining colors (orange, green, and violet). The following are the most-often used configurations for creating color schemes.

Basic Color Wheel

Analogous

Complementary

Split-Complementary

Triad

Tetrad

Complementary Schemes. These are achieved by using two colors that are directly opposite each another on the color wheel. Two such hues are also called contrasting colors. A bright-blue-and-orange bedroom? Well, yes, in full intensity that combination of these two contrasting colors might be hard to stomach, but consider a powdery blue room with pale peach-tone accents. The same complements in varying intensities can make an attractive, soothing combination, while equal amounts of both colors create conflicting tension. The dominance of one color, however, helps to settle things down. Complementary schemes tend to be livelier than others. They consist of a pleasing balance of warm and cool. Strong contrasts may need some tempering, which you can apply by adding a lot of neutral surfaces or by starting with a neutral background (walls) and then using complementary accent colors.

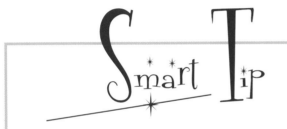

COLOR BASICS. Use color effectively to enhance the perception of the space itself. Make a large room feel cozy with warm colors, which tend to advance. Conversely, open up a small room with cool colors or neutrals, which tend to recede. The less-intense version of a color will generally reduce its tendency to advance or recede, as well. Other tricks: Sharp contrasts often have the same impact as a dark color, reducing perceived space. Monochromatic schemes enlarge space. Neutrals of similar value make walls appear to retreat.

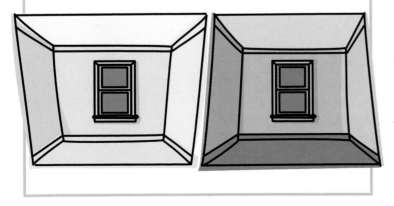

Triadic Schemes. These consist of three or more colors equidistant on the color wheel. Imagine a nursery decorated in palest pink, blue, and yellow. True primaries of red, blue, and yellow often dominate preschoolers' rooms, where everything from toys to storage accessories comes in these colors.

Split-Complementary Schemes. These come together when you combine one color with the colors on both sides of the first color's complementary colors. An example is the combination of violet with orange-yellow and yellow-green.

Tetrad Schemes. These are composed by combining any two pairs of complementary colors — for example, orange and blue with red and green.

So far, you've been thinking about color in terms of personal preference, but there are other things to keep in mind when making a choice. First, color has a psychology about it. For example, warm hues (red, yellow, orange, peach, and cream) tend to energize the atmosphere. They're good choices in places where there's a lot of activity. Cool hues (blue, violet, and green) are more restful. They work well in a room intended for relaxing and unwinding. Your child will play and sleep in his room, so try to find a pleasing balance of both types in your scheme, taking your child's personality into account as well. If he's on the busy side and finds it hard to settle down at nap time, predominantly warm hues may be too stimulating. A restful blue or a calming green may be a better choice in this case.

LIGHT AND COLOR

Lighting can alter color dramatically. The quality of natural light changes through the course of the day, too. Consider this when you choose color for your child's room. Paint some test samples on the wall, and watch how the colors shift throughout the day. Do they need adjustment? Rooms with northern exposures will be filled with bluer, cooler light, which weakens warm colors but intensifies cool hues. Rooms with windows that face south will have a warmer, yellowish light. Rooms with windows that face east are sunny in the morning, while those with a western exposure bring in the late afternoon light.

Of course, you can alter these effects with window treatments and artificial light. These generalizations are not absolute, but they're good starting points for making initial judgments.

In a room with high ceilings, large-scale, repeated shapes help link such diverse designs as the rug and walls in this room.

Pattern

You can add pattern to your child's room in a variety of ways — wallpaper and fabric being the two most popular. Because pattern is largely a vehicle for color, the same rules that guide the selection of color effectively narrow the field when it comes to choosing a pattern or a complement of patterns. Scale, as discussed in Chapter One, is the other important consideration.

Large-scale patterns are like warm colors in that they appear to come toward you. They can create a lively and stimulating atmosphere and generally make a large space seem cozier. In a small room, handle a large-scale pattern with care if you don't want to overpower the space — or your child. That doesn't mean rule it out completely, but perhaps use it more sparingly. Small-scale patterns appear to recede, making small spaces seem larger. These can also be used effectively to camouflage odd angles or corners such as eaves. Try a subtle, nondirectional

pattern for this kind of application. In a large room, the effect of a small pattern can be bland. From a distance it may read as a single color. If you're using a small-scale pattern in a large space, pick one with vibrant colors. For interest, try to vary the scale of patterns. In general, use large-print fabrics on similar-scale furnishings, medium prints on medium-size pieces, and small prints on accent items. Rules, however, can always be broken. Case in point: You want to include a large uphol-stered chair in your teenage daughter's relatively small room. Choose a small print to de-emphasize the scale of the piece. Conversely, you found a terrific but small, old ottoman at a garage sale that would make a unique accent piece in the room. Cover it in a large-scale print fabric to call attention to it. When you think about it, applying the ideas of scale and proportion to pattern selection is really a matter of using your own common sense.

HOW TO MIX PATTERNS

It's not as difficult to mix patterns as it looks, especially if you shop for coordinated lines of fabric and wallpaper, which take the guesswork — and the intimidation—out of using more than one pattern in a room. If you prefer to mix your own patterns, provide links with scale, color, and motif. The regu-larity of checks, stripes, textural looks, and geometrics (if they are small and low-contrast) tends to make them easy-to-mix "neutrals." A small checked pattern can play off a thin ticking stripe, while a strong plaid may require a bolder stripe as a same-scale foil. The most-effective link is shared colors or a similar level of intensity between the prints. A solid-color companion print that pulls out a hue that is shared by more than one pattern provides another way of connecting them.

The twin twig headboards, exposed rafters and beams, plus strong colors and graphic patterns create a whimsical, rustic look in a child's retreat.

Texture

Texture doesn't have the obvious impact on a room that color and pattern wield. But how a material feels, as well as how it looks, is important. The easiest way to incorporate texture into a design is with fabric. Obviously, you won't be using brocades and damasks in your child's room; you'll want something that's sturdy and washable but soft to the touch. Cottons and chenilles are good choices for curtains and bedding. Fabrics, however, are just the beginning. Tactile interest or texture can emanate from any material that is coarse or smooth, hard or soft, matte or shiny, but you should avoid anything that is very rough and can injure a child. Coarse and matte surfaces, such as some carpeting and cork, absorb light and sound. Glossy and smooth surfaces, which range from metal and glass to silk and enamel, reflect light.

Texture affects a room spatially, as well. Coarse or matte surfaces will make a room seem smaller and cozier. The glossy surfaces of some contemporary bedroom furniture can seem cold and uninviting without a cozy quilt on the bed to add warmth and contrast. Smooth and shiny surfaces do the reverse — they make a room seem large and brighter. A room that feels too confined, for instance, may benefit from the addition of a large mirror or a light-color floor. Light reflected off either one will brighten the room.

Keep in mind that texture also affects pattern and color. With fabrics, texture can either soften or enhance a pattern. A coarsely textured surface tones down the intensity of a paint color, and it gives the color more subtle variations. High-gloss surfaces increase the intensity of a color.

Relatively featureless rooms can be improved by adding contrasting textures with wallpaper, paint finishes, or architectural embellishments such as cornices, crown moldings, and wainscoting.

Window treatments are another natural outlet for texture. Fabric choices for draperies and curtains as well as the fabrics and other materials available for blinds and shades are enormous and varied. Texture can be enhanced by the way fabric is hung. Pleating, for example, creates a play of light and shadow. You can combine layers of fabric, or fabric with blinds or shades, to show off different textures.

On the floor, carpets can be smooth, knobby, sculpted, or flecked for visual texture. Rugs, wood, or cork are warming texture options. Varying the materials can make the overall effect more interesting.

Soft cotton chenille fabric on the bed combines with light colors and curvaceous shapes to dress up a teenage girl's room.

Pulling It All Together

How do you go from analyzing the room and your child's needs to choosing the right colors, deciding where to use them, picking out a wallpaper pattern, and selecting fabric? Take it slowly and in steps.

ONE: **Create a sample board.** Use white foam-core presentation board that's sold in art-supply stores. One that measures $8^1/_2$ x 11 inches is ideal. Glue swatches of fabric, paint-color chips, and wallpaper samples to it. Designate about two-thirds of it for the wall and window treatments, and divide the remaining third between the furnishings (including bed linens) and flooring. Add and remove things as you experiment with different looks, and look at the sample board at different times of the day, under various light conditions.

TWO: **Develop the color scheme.** Bringing all you now know about color to bear, pick one main hue. Look at its complement or triad on the color wheel, and choose an accent or two. Go to the paint store and get sample color chips of each of the colors in every intensity you can find so that you can play around until you find the right combination that looks pleasing.

THREE: **Get fabric and wallpaper samples.** You can often pull out a main color from these sources. Look at the way they're mixed in the sample books at the store. Professionals get a lot of their ideas by trial and error. Purchase a few samples, and do a little experimentation of your own.

FOUR: **Review the basic principles of scale, proportion, line, balance, harmony, and rhythm.** If you keep these in mind along with the physical makeup of the space, you can't go wrong. Here, too, practice makes perfect.

Color was a great decorating tool for creating ambience and personality in this child's room, but there's something else that completes the environment—the varied patterns as suggested by the walls, ceiling, and floor, as well as the texturous qualities of other materials: the wicker, fabric, and carpeting.

The sample board will show you at a glance how your choices for wallpaper, fabric and paint will look together. Use it to coordinate the various decorating elements. Add and subtract swatches and samples. You can experiment with different looks.

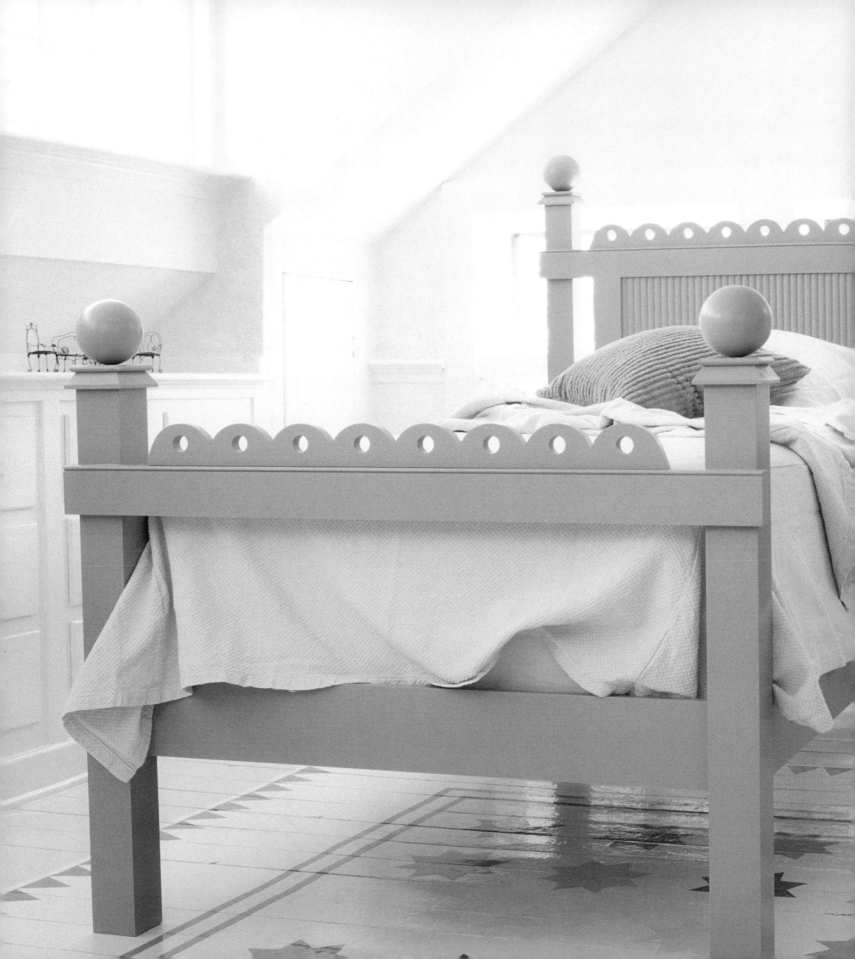

Furnishing Your Child's Room

You'll want furniture that adds style to your child's room, while addressing his practical needs. Of course, in addition to a comfortable crib or bed, your child will need lots of storage. Chapters 5 through 8 will indicate the furniture requirements pertinent to specific age categories. This chapter will cover all of the general information you should know in order to shop for and choose furniture wisely. The first part will discuss beds and bedding; the second part will address storage. Next, you'll find useful information and important facts about lighting and lighting fixtures.

When you're considering furniture, keep in mind that there are small-scaled pieces (including upholstered items) that are specially designed for young children. But for most parents, the more practical choice is furniture that can grow with a child, such as a dressing table that can be converted into a chest of drawers or standard-size furniture that will last through the teen years and into adulthood. You might consider mixing different sizes and kinds of furniture in the room. For example, you could include a small table and chairs or a tot-sized upholstered piece in your design. A small wardrobe with reachable shelves, hooks, and a hanging bar is another practical option. You can't expect a child to hang up her clothes if she can't reach the clothes rod.

The pretty painted cottage-style bed adds youthful appeal to this bedroom. It also establishes a style for the room from which everything else takes its cue. Along with a good, sturdy bed frame, it features a quality mattress and box spring.

A beautiful bed is typically the focal point in a girl's room. A lace-trimmed canopy, right, heightens the drama. A bow, below right, softens the wood headboard with a pretty detail.

As with so many other decorating questions, the answer is always a personal one. Do what you feel is ultimately the best for your child, the physical space, and how much you can afford to spend on furnishings and accessories.

Sleeping Arrangements

Newborns often feel more secure in a cozy bassinet until they are ready to move into a full-size crib, which is usually after a few months. (Refer to Chapter 5, "The Nursery — Baby's First Room," beginning on page 74, for advice about how to select and outfit a crib.) Around the age of two, most children are ready to take the big step of sleeping in a bed, although this change may take place earlier or later. You'll know when the time is right by observing your child. Typically, the signal is when he climbs out of the crib on his own. In general, the Sleep Products Safety Council recommends making the transition from crib to bed once a child is 35 inches tall.

When you shop, select a bed and mattress wisely. These major purchases will affect both the comfort and safety of your child.

BEDS AND MATTRESSES

Along with proper nutrition and exercise, a good night's sleep is essential for your child's well being. Kids do a lot of important things while they're asleep: growing, building new cells, energizing their organs and muscles, and processing all that they have learned today while improving their brain's capacity to learn more tomorrow. If kids don't sleep well, they'll be cranky, less motivated, tired, and

stressed out — the same way you feel when you haven't had enough rest. One way to make sure your child gets proper sleep is with a quality bed and mattress. There are various things to look for when shopping for one.

Beds and mattresses come in different styles and price ranges. While price isn't always an indication of quality, it's fair to assume that if something is cheap, the manufacturer skimped somewhere along the line. And there's one area you should never skimp on: the quality of the mattress. Here's how you can find good quality that's affordable.

 ONE: **Shop for support.** According to the Better Sleep Council, a good mattress and foundation should support the spine along its natural curve. Take your child with you when you shop. Have her lie down on the mattress with a pillow under her head; then slip your hand, palm-side down, under her back. A gap indicates that the mattress is too hard; having to force your hand under the child's back is a sign that the mattress is too soft.

TWO: **Ask about coil count.** It's the number of innersprings (coils) that determine support and durability in a mattress. The larger the bed (ranging from twin-size through king-size), the more coils. For a twin-size mattress, shop for one with at least 200 coils; adequate coil count for a double-size mattress is 300. Better ones have a coil count around 550; the coil count for a top-of-the-line mattress is 700.

THREE: **Compare upholstery options.** Upholstery greatly influences the cost of a mattress and how cushiony or soft it feels. It doesn't affect the more important issue of support, however. Expensive mattresses typically feature fiber-filled cushions; more affordable are those with good-quality, high-density foam, cotton, or wool.

FOUR: **Inquire about materials.** According to the Better Sleep Council, only "29 states and the District of Columbia have laws requiring mattress manufacturers to identify mattresses constructed with new materials." That means that unless you see that assurance on the label, ask your retailer about it; make sure that the sleep set (mattress and foundation) you purchase is new and not refurbished.

FIVE: **Ask the salesperson to explain the warranty.** Of course, the older the mattress, the less support you'll receive from it. Don't expect a mattress to last more than about a dozen years. (Some health experts think you should make a change every 7 years.) A warranty will protect you only against poor workmanship and defects.

Many parents are choosing double beds for their kids today, even when the room isn't shared. This is a practical choice, particularly as children get older and want to have friends over;

MATTRESSES. Even if you're recycling an old bed, buy a new mattress and foundation (typically a box spring), for the sake of cleanliness and your child's orthopedic health. An old mattress is already molded to the previous user's shape, and although it may look clean, it probably harbors dust mites and bacteria no matter how carefully it was maintained.

It's not a good idea to use a new mattress over an old foundation. You may actually shorten the life span of the mattress this way. Mattress and foundation sets are designed to work together for your comfort, so don't try to save a few dollars by buying one and not the other.

If you're considering an antique bed, be prepared to pay for a custom-made mattress and foundation. Today's standard-size mattresses and foundations probably won't fit your vintage bed. Check the measurements of the bed ahead of time.

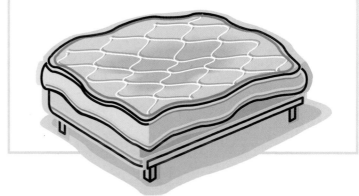

A variety of bed styles lets you choose one for its looks as well as its practical attributes. A painted iron bed, left, suits a Victorian inspired room; a daybed, below, provides extra seating for a teenager's friends; a log-style bunk bed, bottom, lends rustic charm to a boy's room.

the larger bed offers extra seating and lounging space for playing games, listening to music, or watching TV. Another option is a daybed with a trundle or pop-up mattress that rolls under the bed when not in use. This type of bed is popular with teenagers because it can be used as a sofa, as well.

When two children share a room, it's better to have a separate bed for each one. If there isn't room for two twin-size beds, bunk beds offer a solution. Another space-saving idea is a loft bed, which typically features a twin-size bed that is elevated off the floor and rests on a platform. These beds are versatile: Some models also come in double and queen sizes. You can pair a

A coronet-style canopy enveloping this iron daybed adds an air of charming fantasy to a young girl's room.

loft bed with a standard twin-size bed that can slip under the loft to create an L-shaped arrangement in a room. Other types may have built-in storage, a desk, or a playhouse underneath.

Beds come in numerous furniture styles and finishes. Check the frame and construction, and look for safety labels. Run your hand around the frame and headboard to feel for sharp edges, harmful protrusions, or chips or nicks in the finish. Make sure there are no gaps between the mattress, headboard, and frame that are wide enough for little fingers to get caught. Shake the frame and any rails to test for sturdiness, and make sure your child's head can't get stuck between spindles in the headboard. For a very young child, you may want to inquire about optional detachable side rails.

With bunk beds or a loft bed, nothing should wobble; periodically examine all of the bolts and screws, and tighten them immediately if they're loose. Check that the ladder is securely attached to the top bed and that it's at a comfortable angle for climbing. Always install a guardrail on any side that isn't against a wall. Note the headroom. A child on the top bunk should be able to sit up comfortably without hurting himself; likewise a child in the bottom bed should be able to sit up without hitting his head on the bed above him.

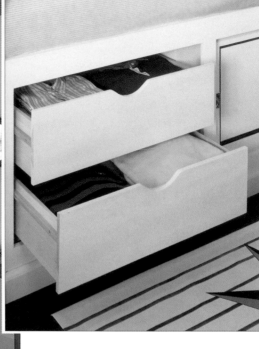

A custom-made built-in bed, left, features bookshelves and lighting. Drawer storage, above, is concealed behind sliding doors.

A sports-car-themed boy's room, below, comes fully loaded with a "racer" bed.

Good-quality beds are constructed with sturdy metal or wood frames. Models made of particleboard are less expensive, but you get what you pay for. In the case of some whimsical styles, such as the "sports car" bed, it makes sense to pay less because your child will outgrow the novelty of it in a few years anyway. However, a well-built one can be passed along to the next child.

Some beds come with built-in storage, either in the headboard or underneath the frame. Drawers that slide out from under the bed are usually deep and wide, which means they can hold bulky items such as extra pillows, blankets, and quilts. But they also take up floor space when they're pulled out, so take this into account when shopping. Take your measuring tape along when you're shopping; pull out the drawers to see how far into the room they'll protrude.

Headboards and Footboards. They're optional, but they help to establish style. In most cases, the bed is the room's focal point — the most dominant feature because it's often the largest object in it. A handsome headboard, with or without a matching footboard, can make a dramatic or whimsical design statement that sets the tone for the entire room.

You can purchase a matching headboard (and footboard) when you buy a suite of coordinated bedroom furniture, but it's more interesting to choose something different. Handsome pairings might include a painted metal bed with laminate storage pieces; iron with mellow maple or oak; or wicker with painted wood. By mixing finishes and materials this way, you're adding textural variety — a sophisticated decorating ploy in any room of the house.

Basic bedstead styles include solid, carved, or curved panels, spindles, slats, spokes, or posts. Spindles and spokes can be short or tall (called a "tester bed"), and a canopy frame can be attached, if desired. Others can be upholstered or feature open or enclosed storage compartments. You can also create your own unique style bedstead with draped fabric, a folding screen, large pillows, painted fence pickets, or anything else you can think of. And, unlike mattresses and foundations, you can recycle an old headboard, refinishing it with a pretty paint technique or decorative finish, such as decoupage. See page 132 in Chapter 8, for more easy how-to instructions for refinishing an old headboard with creative paint-and-paper techniques.

Case Goods

Storage furniture, referred to as case goods in the furniture industry, is available as built-in, modular, or freestanding units. Before you make up your mind about any of these options, it's a good idea to shop around, compare prices, and think hard about your son or daughter's storage needs, always erring on

Built-in storage frames a window in this girl's room, above. All the cabinetry was finished to coordinate with the sleigh bed, below.

the side of too much rather than too little. You might also consider how long you plan to use the furniture; will this be an investment that has to last from early childhood through the teen years and, perhaps, into college? How much abuse do you think it will have to take, and how much time are you willing to take to maintain it? If you know the furniture is going to take a beating, but has to last, invest in something that's well-constructed and has a tough finish.

BUILT-IN FURNITURE

Built-in furniture offers a good solution for an oddly shaped room, in particular, because you can have it custom-designed for the space. This kind of made-to-measure storage also allows you to tailor the cabinet interiors to suit your child's particular storage needs. If he requires racks to hold sporting equipment, your carpenter or contractor can outfit a special cabinet for the purpose, for example. However, custom-made furniture can be expensive. It's a good idea to get several estimates before hiring

someone to build it for you. Get references, preferably from people you know, who have worked with the person, and ask to see examples of his or her work.

One way you might be able to save some money is if you purchase stock cabinetry that can be retrofitted into the space, just like kitchen cabinetry. In fact, you should price stock kitchen cabinets, especially discontinued lines that are often discounted. But speak to your contractor or carpenter about this before buying to make sure this plan is feasible.

MODULAR SYSTEMS

Like modular seating, modular storage systems consist of separate, coordinated units that can be purchased individually or as an entire suite. Modular systems have the look of built-in furniture but, unless custom-made, they're usually more affordable. Of course, price is determined by the number of pieces and the finish that you choose, and whether assembly is needed.

Made-to-measure furniture was the solution in this oddly shaped room, left. Coordinated modular units, below, fit into the floor plan of another room.

Modular furniture can be used to create storage walls or room dividers, and it comes in handy when you have to divide up the space of one room for two children. Storage walls are connected units that fit from floor to ceiling. They divide space while providing access to storage from one or both sides. Room dividers serve a similar purpose, but do not extend to the ceiling or even from wall to wall.

It's best to purchase this type of furniture after you've seen it yourself in a showroom. Check for sturdiness and that hinges and supports are strong. Run your hands across the finish to make sure that it's smooth. Especially if the furniture is for a

Bookshelves and drawer storage were built around two twin-size beds, above, to give each of the room's occupants an equal amount of storage. The parents chose simple styling so that the furniture wouldn't look dated or out of place when the décor is changed later.

nursery or a young child's room, inspect it for sharp corners and edges; choose pieces with rounded corners whenever possible. Examine the shelving. It should be strong enough to hold a large amount of books, and adjustable so that you can install it at a safe and comfortable height for your child. Avoid anything with glass doors. Even if it's shatterproof, kids will be kids, and you'll be wiping off smudges and sticky fingerprints from glass all the time. Glass isn't for kids' rooms.

If you have to assemble the furniture yourself, ask the salesperson whether you need better-than-average skills and what tools are required. If the furniture comes in pieces in boxes ready to be carried away, can you fit the boxes into your car? Sometimes you can pay the store for assembly, but that could mean you must have the furniture delivered — for another fee.

FREESTANDING FURNITURE

Generally, dressers and chests are categorized by the size of their contents. The smallest is a lingerie chest followed by the drawer chest. The door chest is larger still with drawers at the bottom and two doors at the top. The armoire, or wardrobe, is the largest "chest" available. A clothes rod inside defines it as a wardrobe. In your child's bedroom, you might also

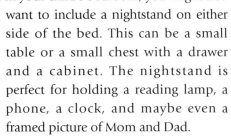

want to include a nightstand on either side of the bed. This can be a small table or a small chest with a drawer and a cabinet. The nightstand is perfect for holding a reading lamp, a phone, a clock, and maybe even a framed picture of Mom and Dad.

Depending on the size of the room, other options include open shelves, cabinets with hinged or sliding doors, and drawers in many shapes and sizes. Storage pieces also offer areas for the display or protection of collectibles and other valuables. Almost every child has a collection of something; it could be dolls, stuffed animals, ceramic pieces, seashells, sports memorabilia, funny hats, or anything thing else that expresses your son or daughter's favorite things.

This colorful bookcase is whimsical in appearance but very practical in terms of storage. Use it to hold toys, books, extra toss pillows, and just about anything that will fit on a shelf.

CASE GOODS. The furniture industry uses a variety of labels to denote the materials used in a piece of case-goods furniture. The meanings of these labeling terms are regulated by the Federal Trade Commission.

▶ *Solid wood* (i.e., "solid oak" or "solid pine") means that the exposed surfaces are made of this wood without any veneer or plywood. Other woods may be used on unexposed surfaces such as drawer sides and backs.

▶ *Genuine wood* means that all exposed parts of the furniture are made of a veneer of the wood named, over hard-wood plywood.

▶ *Wood* means that none of the parts of the furniture are made of plastic, metal, or other materials.

▶ *Man-made materials* refers to plastic laminate panels that are printed to look like wood. The furniture may also include plastic molded to look like wood carving or trim.

Built to last through childhood, quality wood furniture features strong construction, particularly at the joints. The spindles on these beds, left, are spaced so that a child's arms and legs can't get caught. This wardrobe clothes rack, above, is reachable for kids.

Good Furniture Construction

Furniture can be constructed of hardwood or softwood. Hardwoods are from deciduous trees, such as cherry, maple, oak, ash, pecan, teak, walnut, mahogany, and poplar. Hardwoods are often used in high-quality furniture because they are stronger than softwoods. Softwoods are from conifer trees, such as fir, pine, redwood, cedar, and cypress. The wood has to be well-seasoned and kiln-dried before it is put to use or it will split and splinter easily.

Veneers are thin sheets of hardwood that are glued to a core of less expensive material. Once associated with poor-quality furniture, veneers are more acceptable today and may be stronger than solid wood. Wide boards of solid wood will warp and crack with weather changes; veneer over plywood won't.

The "solid wood" label allows use of composition boards, such as plywood and particleboard, in nonexposed areas of the furniture. You will find these materials used this way in medium-priced furniture. In budget-priced furniture, they may be used extensively.

JOINING METHODS

Wood can be joined together with staples, nails, screws, joints, and glue. Several of these methods may be used in one piece of furniture. To evaluate quality, look for strong construction at the joints. Joints are where one part of a piece of furniture fits into another. They're usually glued together with synthetic glues or fastened with screws. Staples are used only on the most inexpensive furniture and should not be used to join any piece that bears weight. Nails are stronger than staples but not as strong as the following joining methods. If you intend to make a quality furniture purchase, look for them.

Butt joints connect the edge of one piece of wood to the face of another. They are weak joints, and should be used only in places that are not subject to stress, such as where a bureau top meets the frame. Using *dowels* makes stronger butt joints.

Dovetail joints are used to join drawer sides. Notches cut into the ends of each piece should fit together smoothly.

Double-dowel joints use two dowels to peg joints together. These are extremely sturdy joints. They are used in case-goods framing and to attach legs to the side rails of chairs.

Mortise-and-tenon joinery is the strongest method of joining pieces of wood at right angles. The end of one piece of wood is shaped to fit into a hole in the other, which distributes weight or stress over a wide area.

Corner blocks may be set into joints and screwed in place to provide extra support.

FINISHES

Finishes can add color and protection through the use of stains, paints, or lacquers. A clear finish will allow the natural grain of wood to show through, while wood stains will change the color of the wood. Finishes can make a piece of furniture look smooth or rustic.

A clear finish on this furniture allows the natural appearance of the wood to show through while adding protection. The storage shelves, right, put most toys within easy reach.

Miter joints are used at the corners of tables. The ends of the two pieces are angled to fit together at right angles. This joint should be reinforced with dowels, nails, or screws.

Tongue-and-groove joints are used to join two or more boards together side by side, as in a tabletop. A groove is cut into one side of a board and a tongue carved out on the other. When placed side by side, the tongue of one board fits into the groove of the next and so on.

Distressing is a popular means of making new wood look old. The wood is beaten and battered before the finish is applied, "aging" it and enhancing its rustic charm. These finishes tend to hide any scratches or fingerprints the furniture may be exposed to and make good choices for kids' rooms, where they're liable to take a beating.

Painted finishes, which are popular today, can be playful or artful. Unlike a distressed finish, however, paint tends to highlight flaws in the wood. This makes painted pieces more expensive than ones with natural finishes because extra care must be taken at the factory to remove imperfections from the wood. If you plan to refinish an old piece of wood furniture, you can do the work yourself to save money. Depending on the shape it's in, wood furniture requires various levels of skills to restore it. Sometimes all it takes is re-gluing loose joints, filling in small nicks with wood filler, a light sanding, and a new stain or painted finish.

Finishes are definitely a matter of personal taste, but should always be strong enough to resist moisture. Inexpensive pieces may be simply coated with a layer of polyurethane. The finishing of high-quality furniture includes sanding, glazing, waxing, and hand buffing. Become familiar with different finishes by comparing the look and feel between inexpensive and expensive pieces. Always check that the surface is hard, smooth, and even. Watch for uneven colorations, bubbles, or cracks in the surface.

Upholstered Furniture

If you have the space, it's nice to include a comfortable upholstered piece in the bedroom. Whether you're thinking of a window seat, an armchair and ottoman, a petite slipper chair, or even a small sofa or love seat, you should shop armed with some information about upholstery.

When you buy upholstered furniture, you can often choose from a range of price levels, called *grades*, of fabric or coverings. These grades are assigned a letter from A to D on up, with A at the high-price end. Grading is determined by the quality of the materials, the amount of fabric needed to match the pattern at the seams, corners, and edges, and the source of the pattern

FURNITURE QUALITY. When shopping for case goods, you'll find varying levels of quality and pricing. Use this checklist to judge what you're getting for your money.

▶ Veneers and laminates should be joined well to the base material.

▶ Cabinet doors should work smoothly.

▶ Hinges and other hardware should be strong and secure.

▶ Drawers should fit well, glide easily, and have stops.

▶ Bottoms of drawers should be held by grooves, not staples or nails.

▶ Insides of drawers should be smooth and sealed.

▶ Corners of drawers should have dovetail joints.

▶ Joints bearing weight should be reinforced with corner blocks.

▶ Back panels should be screwed into the frame.

▶ Finish should feel smooth (unless it is distressed).

▶ Long shelves should have center supports.

Contrast piping on this colorfast cushion fabric adds a little extra to the cost, but a lot to the style of this window seat.

design (a famous designer's pattern costs more). Luckily, upholstered furniture in this room won't be subjected to much of the hard use it would get in another room in the house, such as the family room, so you may not have as much concern for structural elements (the frame, legs, arms). However, because upholstery coverings affect the price of furniture more than any other element of construction, keep the following in mind if you want to trim the cost of your furniture.

✱ *Frame design:* Curves are more expensive to cover than straight lines.

✱ *Pattern design:* Large, complex patterns are harder to match than small, overall designs.

✱ *Details:* Pleats, welts, braids, buttons, and fringe all add to the final cost.

An important factor to consider when selecting upholstery fabric is durability. In general, tightly woven fabrics wear best. Fabrics with woven-in patterns wear better than printed fabrics. Various natural and synthetic fibers offer different looks and textures and perform differently in terms of wear and tear. In a child's room, it makes sense to use a fabric that has been treated for stain resistance at the mill. Any coating that you can spray

The woven fabric on this armchair, left, wears well. A slipcover, such as the one on the love seat, above, is practical because it can be washed.

on with a can will come off when you wash or even spot-clean the fabric. (You can re-treat the fabric with the spray-on product yourself, after cleaning, however.)

Natural fibers include cotton, linen, wool, and silk. Cotton is soft and durable. However, its fibers will disintegrate under consistent exposure to direct sunlight. Keep that in mind if you're covering a window seat that's exposed to strong, direct sunlight. Cotton is also less stain resistant than synthetic fibers. Linen has a tailored, crisp feel and is one of the most durable fibers available. It is most often found in natural colors because it does not dye well. It, too, disintegrates in sunlight. Wool is extremely durable as well as abrasion- and stain-resistant, but should be mothproofed before use. Silk is a beautiful, but fragile fabric. Soft and luxurious, it is difficult to clean and discolors under strong light. For all of these reasons, it's not a good choice for a child's room.

Synthetic fibers have been developed as alternatives to natural fibers and are often blended with them. Polyester is strong and easy to clean. It withstands direct sunlight and is flame- and abrasion-resistant. Rough in texture, it is often blended with natural fibers to soften its touch. It is a smart choice for a kid's room. On the other hand, olefin is used to create heavy textured fabrics. It is a coarse and bulky fiber that is strong and stain-resistant. However, it does not wear well under direct sunlight. Nylon is the strongest and most soil-resistant fiber. Recent developments in nylon give it the look and feel of wool. It, too, is sensitive to sunlight.

When shopping for fabric or buying upholstered furniture, read labels and make sure all material is flame resistant.

Lamps and Other Lighting Fixtures

Don't forget to include thoughtful lighting fixtures in your plans. For the best result, become familiar with the basic concepts behind good lighting design.

There are three types of lighting to consider in any room design: ambient, task, and accent lighting. For the safety and comfort of your son or daughter's room, pay special attention to ambient lighting, which is the general illumination that fills the entire room. Task lighting, which brightens a specific area, such as a desktop is also paramount, especially as children begin to read and do projects in their rooms. Accent lighting is purely decorative; you can use it to spotlight a framed print on the wall or to highlight a collection that's displayed on a shelf, for example.

In a nursery or very young child's room, you'll want lighting that works for you and your tot. You'll spend a lot of time there, helping him or her to dress, reading stories, and cuddling.

Accent lighting can be inventive. Note that the city skyline in this dramatic mural is actually lit! It's a fun part of the stimulating backdrop for the room's creative environment.

A dimmer switch is a great idea: You can use it to brighten light when attending to the baby and then to adjust the light to a lower level for nighttime needs.

Over time, your child's individual requirements for playing, studying, and doing hobbies will develop. Lighting that supports these more demanding visual tasks is important in order to avoid eyestrain.

AMBIENT AND TASK LIGHTING

Wall sconces, recessed fixtures, and track lighting are excellent sources of ambient light. They're also probably the safest kinds of fixtures to use in a young child's room. With them, you don't have to worry about lamps tipping over when kids get rambunctious. Keeping any source of light out of reach for little hands can prevent burns.

Recessed fixtures combined with an adjustable arm or gooseneck desk lamp are a perfect combination in the work area

Wall sconces in this teenager's room, above left, offer soft, flattering illumination at the vanity table.

A ceiling-mounted fixture is practical for general lighting needs in a nursery, especially when it can be controlled by a dimmer switch.

because you can control glare and balance the general light with them. Never aim any light source directly onto the desk or work surface; angle it to avoid eye-straining glare.

Any lamp that's used in a child's room has to be designed so that it doesn't tip easily or produce high levels of heat that can be dangerous. Look for lamps that are not top heavy, are generally well-balanced, or can clip securely onto a desk. (Avoid floor lamps, which can be easily knocked over.) Opt for bright general lighting for kids who play on the floor during the early years. Add localized task lighting where children read, draw, or do crafts. When kids are old enough to read in bed, an adjustable light near the bedpost is a good idea. Besides, a lamp near the bed makes it safer for kids who sometimes have to get up during the night. Night lights along the way to the bathroom are always helpful as well, especially to prevent tripping over toys and other items left on the floor. At the computer, provide both task and general lighting that is compatible with the screen at the child's height. The idea is to illuminate what is displaced on the monitor with task lighting, while using ambient light to eliminate the distracting contrast of what's on the screen and the area behind it.

READING IN BED

You can encourage your kids to read more if you make it comfortable to do so. Children are lower to the mattress than adults when it comes to reading. Adjustable lamp arms should be positioned best to meet a child's needs. As kids get bigger,

An adjustable lamp at this desk, below, can easily be directed for a glare-free illumination of the work surface. A reading light, below right, is installed at a comfortable height for the room's young occupant.

other types of fixtures are fine, but they must meet certain criteria.

For example, bedside table lamps should be no more than 32 inches high for comfort. The lamp should have a shade with a bottom circumference of 15 to 17 inches, a top circumference of 8 to 15 inches, and a depth from top to bottom of 6 to 14 inches. For reading comfort, the lamp should line up with your child's shoulder (when he or she is propped up in a reading position), 22 inches to the side of the book's center, and with the bottom of the shade about 20 to 24 inches from the top of the mattress.

Wall-mounted or hanging lamps are another option; they make the most of a tight space. Position them as you would a bedside table lamp (see above).

DRESSER AND VANITY LAMPS

When you're selecting lamps for a child's dresser or vanity, you'll want ones that are stylish and practical. If the lamps are for a large dresser with a mirror that will be used by an older child for grooming, select fixtures that measure 25 inches measured from the dresser top to the center of the shade. Generally, the shade's bottom circumference should be 11 to 14 inches, with a top circumference of 7 to 8 inches, and a depth of at least 7 to 9 inches from the top of the shade to the bottom.

Multi-task lighting is required in an older child's room. Here, a floor lamp provides over-the-shoulder light for reading while small vanity lamps assist grooming.

You'll have to scale down for grooming while seated at a vanity or dressing table. Select lamps that are 15 inches from the tabletop to the center of the shade. The best shade dimensions for this situation are a bottom that's 9 to 11 inches, a top minimum of 7 to 8 inches, and a depth of 9 inches. The bulb should be at least 2 inches below the top of the shade so that you don't look into it when you're standing.

Although a reading lamp can use 60- to 75-watt bulb, double dressers and large dressing tables require broader lamps that are in scale and produce more light. These lamps may take up to 100 or 150 watts to make grooming easy to see.

If you carefully consider all of the room's lighting requirements, you'll realize that choosing the right fixture is more than a matter of style. Besides, lamps come in every style: traditional, country, or contemporary. After you've decided on lighting, you're ready to explore the options presented in the next chapter, "Walls, Windows, & Floors."

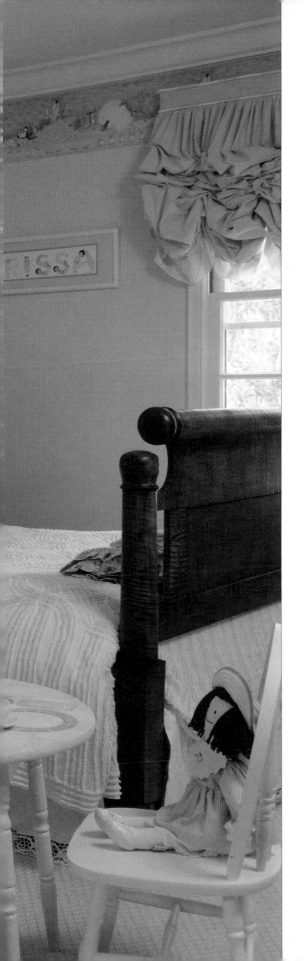

Walls, Windows & Floors

*O*ne of the easiest ways to transform any space in the house into a personality-packed room for a child of any age is with new wall and window treatments. Add attractive flooring, and you've tied all of the surfaces together nicely. Wall, window, and floor treatments also provide a perfect opportunity for adding color, pattern, and texture to the room's design. In most cases, these are reasonably affordable home improvements that you can make yourself. Painting and installing wallpaper are relatively easy projects that you can complete over a weekend. Putting in new flooring or wall-to-wall carpeting are jobs best left to a professional, however.

The way to start is by looking at what's on the market and deciding on the design you and your child would like to achieve. If you don't want to redecorate often, look for wallpaper patterns or colors that are suitable for boys or girls and aren't too juvenile. Avoid faddish cartoon or toy-inspired themes, which tend to become dated quickly — sometimes within a few months. Stick with classic motifs and colors if you want to be on the safe side. Besides avoiding themes or palettes that are too trendy, carefully consider maintenance and durability of wallpaper types, fabrics, and flooring materials before buying something just because it looks good. In this chapter, you'll learn about all of the different options that are available, and which ones are best for your project.

A durable vinyl wallpaper that's easy to clean is a good choice in a child's room. The pinstriped pattern, which is topped by a border with a nursery-rhyme theme, will look stylish for years.

This "Cow That Jumped Over The Moon" nursery-rhyme theme on the border adds just the right youthful note. As the child grows older, simply replace the border with one that's more age-appropriate.

Wall Treatments

You have a choice: Decorate the walls to make a dramatic statement, or let them act as an unobtrusive backdrop for the furnishings. If the furniture isn't particularly interesting, add pizzazz to the room with bold colors or patterns; on the other hand, a subtle palette won't take away from a beautiful bed or handsome built-in furniture.

If the room lacks architectural interest, you can create good-looking effects with either paint or wallpaper or a combination of the two. Add a frieze (a band installed on the upper portion of the wall near the ceiling line) or a chair rail using a wallpaper border, for example. Or create a wainscot effect by painting the wall; then install wallpaper on the bottom half of the wall and a border at chair-rail height. You're really only limited by your imagination and how much time and money you have to spend.

PAINT

This is your easiest and least-expensive option. There is nothing like a fresh coat of paint to make a room look clean and new. The important thing to remember when buying paint is that there are different grades. In general, the higher the grade, the better the quality — and the higher the price. Bargain paints aren't always a good deal: They don't offer the coverage that a better-grade product does, and you'll have to make up for that deficiency with additional coats — and extra gallons — of paint; so where's the savings?

Smart Tip

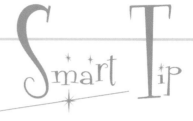

PAINT BASICS. Most interior paints are either *alkyd-resin* (oil-based) products or *latex* (water-based) varieties. Oil and water don't mix, and generally neither do the paints based on them. For multilayered effects, stick to one type or the other.

▶ Alkyd paints are somewhat lustrous, translucent, and hardwearing. But alkyds, and the solvents needed for cleaning up, are toxic and combustible, requiring good work-site ventilation. Alkyds are better suited to special techniques such as combing and ragging, where glaze is brushed on in sections and then manipulated to create texture and special effects.

▶ Latex paints, which now approach alkyd's durability and textural range, are nontoxic, quick-drying, and they clean up easily with soap and water. Most nonprofessionals find latex paint easier to deal with and capable of creating many popular decorative finishes. In general, latex paints are best suited to effects that are dabbed on over the base coat, as in sponging or stenciling. The short drying time can be an advantage because mistakes can be painted over and redone.

Latex paint is usually the best choice for covering an entire wall, because the job can be completed from start to finish in just a few hours or over the course of a day.

Add visual interest to plain surfaces. Above, the ceiling, molding, and walls were painted different colors. Right, paint was used another way to create an imaginative effect. Below right, a wallpaper border was installed at chair-rail height.

Custom colors, the kind you get when you take a swatch of fabric to the paint store and ask to have it matched, will add to the cost, but it's worth it. (Never guess when it comes to color; even slight variations in the tone or shade of one color can clash.) Sheen will raise the price as well; in most cases, a glossy paint is more expensive than one with a flat finish. Designer and specialty paints, those that produce decorative effects or textures, are premium products that sometimes require special application tools as well. You might want to use them sparingly or limit them to trim.

Flat paints are typically best for walls and ceilings, but they tend to mar easily, so you may not want to use them in a young child's room where the walls will get lots of hand marks and other abuse. A semi-gloss finish, which has a higher sheen than a flat finish, will be easier to keep clean because you can wipe off marks with a damp cloth and mild detergent in most cases.

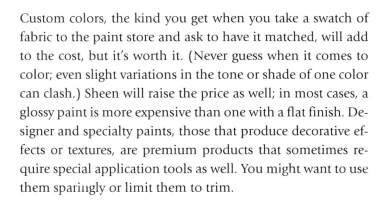

Some paint products are formulated and marketed specifically for kids' rooms, and they let you create fun effects easily and with no particular professional skills. These products include glow-in-the-dark and glittery top coats, as well as blackboard paint that kids can write and draw on, and then erase. Just keep in mind that you may have to give the walls a light sanding before painting over some of these effects when you want to make a change later.

WALLPAPER

Wallpaper can add instant style to your child's room and give you a headstart in developing the overall decorating scheme. Popular patterns include character themes, animals, sports motifs, and other collections that have been designed to appeal to young children. If your son or daughter is beyond this stage, you can select from a wide range of ready-made patterns, which are suitable for any room in the house. In either case, some patterns are designed to coordinate with other prints and matching fabrics so that you can easily mix and match them to create a cohesive look not only for the walls but for window treatments and bed dressing as well. But don't go overboard with mix-and-match prints, or you'll make the room look formulaic.

There are several types of wallcoverings on today's market, but when kids are involved, it's always practical to choose

something that's marked *washable and scrubbable.* Generally, delicate hand-painted wallpapers, natural fabrics or weaves, and flocked or embossed coverings are inappropriate for a child's room.

Vinyl coverings. This is the most popular kind because it can take a beating. Finger marks, grease, and moisture pose no threat to its long-lasting good looks. There are three types for your consideration.

✳ *Paper-backed vinyl* is plenty sturdy for kids' rooms, and it's generally washable and peelable, which means when your daughter gets too old for dancing teddy bears, you can

Coordinating wallpaper and fabrics, left, create a cohesive look in a boy's room. The border in this little girl's room, below, sets the mood for a real tea party.

remove the paper without difficulty. It's frequently sold prepasted, which makes it easier to apply, as well. Fortunately, most wallpaper patterns geared for kids' rooms are printed on paper-backed vinyl.

✳ *Fabric-backed vinyl* has a vinyl top layer over fiberglass or cloth. It's tough, which means you can scrub crayon markings. This type is heavier than paper-backed vinyl, and it doesn't come prepasted.

✳ *Vinyl-coated paper* is inexpensive, but it isn't as durable as the two previously mentioned types. Sticky, oily little hands will permanently mar it.

When you're ready to select a pattern, don't forget the principles of scale and proportion, line, balance, rhythm, and harmony, which were discussed in Chapter 1. You might also review Chapter 2, "Introducing Color, Pattern, and Texture." Naturalistic (floral) and stylized (repeated motif) patterns

Black and white stripes are suitably sophisticated in a teenager's bedroom, above. A floral motif, below, appears more traditionally feminine.

complement traditional schemes that are either formal or casual. Abstract and geometric patterns work well in contemporary settings. These rules are not hard and fast, however. A geometric pattern, such as a plaid, for example, can be very much at home in a traditional or country décor, and stripes look great with just about any decorating style. In most cases, a pattern that's too large for the room will overpower it; a pattern that's too small will seem to fade away. Light or neutral-color backgrounds add an airy look to a small room; dark backgrounds make a large space feel less impersonal and more cozy.

To be on the safe side, it's a good idea to borrow the wallpaper sample book (if the store will allow it) or ask for a small cutting to take home. Better yet, buy one roll. Take a look at the pattern and colors in the room at different times of the day with the lights on and with them off. This is the only way to be sure that the pattern and color you've selected are right for the space.

Borders are paired with wallpaper, typically, but you can use them to dress up a plain painted wall, as well. One trick is to install wallpaper with a basic design, then apply a border that features a strong theme. That way you can retain the wallpaper but replace the border when your child gets older and outgrows a juvenile theme.

Additional special ideas for using wallpaper include

* Setting off special areas with different patterns. Many patterns come in reverse versions (a dark color on a light background versus a light color on a dark background). You could try this in an alcove or eaves to play up the interesting lines created by the architecture.

* Picking a theme that will coordinate easily with the room's other elements, such as the bedding and curtains.

* Preparing the wall properly by sanding and priming so that the wallpaper adheres smoothly and adequately.

Window Treatments

You can accomplish a few objectives with window treatments. First and foremost, use them to strengthen or soften the opening. In other words, you can play up an attractive window (and view), as well as play down one that's less than pleasing. Window treatments also provide an opportunity for introducing more color and pattern into the room, while allowing you to control natural light and provide privacy and insulation. Even if a room has small windows, it can be cheerful and relatively bright if you select the right window treatment; conversely, a room with large drafty windows can be made comfortable when the windows are dressed to keep the cold out but let the sunshine in.

There are lots of types of window treatments to choose from, including many styles of curtains, shades, blinds, and shutters. Usually a combination or layering of two or more provides the most versatility. Pair sheers with lined, adjustable

ESTIMATING WALLPAPER AND PAINT NEEDS. First, determine the room's square footage: Multiply the width and length of the room. For example, if the room is 12 feet wide and 15 feet long, the formula goes like this: 12 x 15 = 180 square feet. Subtract 21 square feet for each standard-size door in the room, 15 square feet for each standard-size window, and the actual square footage of any built-in features, such as bookcases. This gives you the room's *adjusted square footage.*

To estimate how much paint you'll need, first check the labels on paint containers to determine their recommended coverage. Most paints will specify coverage of 350 to 400 square feet per gallon, but it's safer to plan on coverage of 300 square feet per gallon and 75 square feet per quart. Always buy more paint than you need. A general rule of

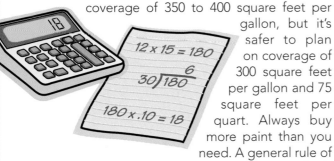

thumb is to add 10 percent to your estimate (multiply the adjusted square footage by 0.10), and then round up to the next highest quart. Don't take a chance on coming up short. If you have to have another gallon of paint mixed later, the color may be slightly different than that of the first batch.

To estimate how much wallpaper you'll need, determine the room's adjusted square footage, and then divide that number by 30; this takes into account the likely wastage from the standard 36 square feet in a roll. Round up to the nearest whole number for ordering standard rolls. For anything else, ask the salesperson to help you. A repeating pattern requires careful planning of where the job should start and end.

Painted effects let you get creative in your child's room. If you're a beginner, choose an easy technique such as stamping or stenciling, and use quick-drying paint. The gold stars were applied to this nursery ceiling with a star-shaped stamp.

Simple tab curtains, left, easily open or close to control light and air. The gingham border matches the crib quilts.

Balloon valances, below, with a ruffled hem add a touch of feminine frill to a little girl's room.

they add a soft, cozy feeling to the room. If lined, curtains can block out drafts and harsh sunlight. Among their disadvantages is that they collect dust and may require professional cleaning; and they have to be completely closed to adequately keep out strong sunlight and cold air.

Blinds. Whether they're made of metal, wood, or vinyl, blinds effectively block the sun when they're closed. Today's many styles include a wide selection of colors, textured-fabric finishes, and the choice of vertical or horizontal slats in standard, mini, or micro widths. You can pair them with curtains or valances, or use them alone to cover a window. They come in standard ready-made sizes, or they can be custom-ordered to fit any size or shape window.

The advantage of blinds is that they are adjustable, which makes it easy to control privacy, light, and air. Their disadvantages include a somewhat sterile appearance unless it's

panels or a simple valance with blinds or shutters. You can purchase them ready-made in standard window sizes or, if your budget allows, custom-order them to the windows' specifications or to match the bedding or wallpaper pattern. In any case, you'll choose from several basic types.

Curtains and Valances. Curtains made from washable fabrics (typically a cotton and polyester blend) are the easiest to care for, but if your child has allergies or a sensitivity to fabric sizing or synthetics, it's wiser to select a fabric that's 100 percent natural. However, cotton curtains have to be lined to be fade-resistant, which is a consideration if the windows receive strong exposure to the sun.

Depending on the decorating style of the room and the size and shape of the windows, you may choose between short or long, ruffled, or plain panels; café styles; sheer or solid fabrics; tab-top, pleated, or gathered headings; and swagged, pouffed, ballooned, or festooned valances. While traditional and country décors can carry off fussier treatments, contemporary-style rooms require the simplicity of a tailored or pared-down treatment.

The advantages of curtains are that you can easily coordinate them with the color or print used on the wall and bed linens;

Handsome wood blinds installed on the French doors lend privacy to this boy's room. The valances are actually Roman shades that can be rolled down for added insulation on cool nights. Wall art sets the sports theme for the room's décor.

Shades come in a variety of styles and materials. Opposite, clockwise from the top: a cloud shade, Roman shades, and a matchstick shade.

softened with the addition of curtains or valances; the slats, which attract dirt, can be awkward to clean.

Shades. Generally considered soft window treatments, shades are made of single pieces of fabric or vinyl attached to a roller and operated with a cord or via a spring mechanism. Fabric shades can be flat, gathered, or pleated. Some shades can block out the sun entirely when they're drawn; others filter it. Use them alone or with curtains. Like blinds, shades come in standard ready-made sizes, or they can be custom-ordered. Popular variations include Roman shades, balloon shades, pleated-fabric shades, and cellular shades.

The advantages of shades include a versatility of styles and colors and their easy operation in controlling light and privacy. Their disadvantages are that they can be difficult to clean; also, they will not block out sunlight unless they are made of a heavy, more costly room-darkening material.

Shutters can be versatile, too. Above, the lower portion of the windows features louvered plantation shutters. Left, café shutters with gingham panels add to an Old West theme.

Shutters. Louvered shutters are made from wood. Open them for air; close them for privacy. They may be painted or stained, and some come with a fabric panel that can be made to match fabric used on other furnishings in the room. Wide louvers have a contemporary appeal; narrow louvers lend a country feeling. You can purchase standard sizes or custom-order shutters to fit your window.

The advantages of shutters are the privacy they offer when closed and the fact that slats can be opened or closed easily to control air and light. Their disadvantage is that they have to be custom-made for oddly shaped or sized windows.

Before you shop for any window treatment, consider the room's needs carefully, and walk yourself through the following Smart Steps.

SMART STEPS

ONE: **Note the room's orientation and view.** Figure out how the room's exposure to the sun at various times of the day will affect its function. A nursery may look lovely with the early morning sun streaming in, but unless you want baby up at dawn each day, you may need to consider a room-darkening treatment if the window faces east. A window that faces west will get most of its sunlight in the afternoon — just in time for naps — while a southern exposure is bright most of the day. Luckily, most window treatments are adjustable and will allow you to control the amount of light you want to filter into the room at different hours of the day. But because north-facing windows receive no direct sunlight, window treatments should be adequately lined with insulating material to keep the room temperature comfortable, especially during the winter months.

TWO: **Choose the proper hardware.** The right rod, pole, clips, or rings are important for the proper installation of a

Attractive details, such as the star holdback, top, or the ribbon tieback, above, dress up plain curtains. Handsome finials on the rods, left, punctuate an animal theme.

window treatment because they support it. True, some window hardware is decorative, but remember the old adage: Form follows function. If you substitute a flimsy metal rod when the installation calls for a substantial wooden pole, the curtain will not hang right. Stylewise, heavy, highly ornamented finials and rods can look out of place and too formal and sophisticated in a young child's room.

THREE: **Decide on an inside or outside mount.** You can install your window treatment inside or outside the window opening, depending on whether or not you want the trim to show. However, the time to make this decision is before you shop for curtains and hardware, when you're taking measurements, not after you've begun the installation.

FOUR: **Measure Up.** Two windows, even if they're in the same room, can have different measurements. Never assume otherwise. Using a steel measuring tape, take the dimensions of every window in the room.

FIVE: **Consider maintenance.** Delicate fabrics and elaborate trims require professional care. You can't throw these materials into the washing machine and dryer. Some custom-made treatments have to be professionally installed and removed, as well. Consider your budget carefully if this is an option.

Flooring

Children of all ages spend a lot of time on the floor: They play, eat, and even sleep on it sometimes. So the flooring material you choose is important. It has to be comfortable and easy to clean. The variety of flooring is great. Innovations in technology have widened the range with finishes that make the most of style and easy maintenance. As you review these options, remember that some can be mixed and matched for an interesting and creative variation that also allows flexibility of design within almost any budget. Also review the earlier discussion of color, which is in Chapter 2.

If the room is small, a light-color floor will make it feel more spacious; if the room is large, a pattern will add coziness. Of course, you should balance what you decide to put on the floor with the colors and patterns on the other surfaces in the room as well.

Good flooring is an investment in your child's room that can last to adulthood, so it's wise to plan for it carefully.

WOOD

Today's manufacturers offer a variety of hardwood flooring, factory- or custom-stained. A traditional favorite, wood flooring is available in strips of 2 to 3 inches wide, or in country-style planks of 10 inches wide or more. The look of a parquet floor is unparalleled for richness of visual texture. Prefinished hardwood tile blocks are now manufactured in a variety of patterns, making parquet possible at a reasonable price.

Softwoods, such as pine and fir, are often used to make simple tongue-and-groove floorboards. Softwoods are less suitable for high-traffic areas but can survive most kids' rooms well. The hardwoods — maple, birch, oak, or ash — are far less likely to mar with normal use, but a hardwood floor is not indestructible; it will stand up to use, but not abuse.

The rug's pretty floral pattern enhances the feminine appeal and coziness of this young girl's room. Its colors echo the hues on the wall, in the bed's coverlet and quilt, and on the window seat.

Color stains — reds, blues, and greens — look great in a kid's room where the overall style of the room is usually casual. Natural wood stains range from very light ash tones to deep, coffee-like colors. Generally, lighter stains make a room feel less formal, and darker, richer stains suggest a traditional atmosphere. Lighter stains — as with lighter colors — create a feeling of openness and make a room look larger; darker stains can make a large, cold space feel warm.

Most wood-flooring installations are by professionals, although some kits are relatively easy for do-it-yourselfers. As for maintenance, a regular vacuum cleaning or dust mopping may be all that's needed if the wood has been sealed properly with polyurethane. You can wash a wood floor as long as you use a product that's manufactured specifically for this purpose; but water and wood are not the best combination. In most cases, you'll want to keep the flooring soft underfoot by adding a rug or carpeting, which will take the brunt of the abuse.

More than one stain was used to create the swirl effect, above, on a child's playroom floor. Large blocks with a small inset block, right, were stenciled onto this wood floor.

Both hardwoods and softwoods are graded according to their color, grain, and imperfections. The top of the line is known as clear, followed by select, Number 1 common, and Number 2 common. In addition to the budget considerations, the decision whether to pay top dollar for clear wood or to economize with a lesser grade depends on use factors and on the design objectives. For example, if you plan to install carpeting or a rug over the wood flooring, the Number 2 common grade is a practical choice. Another factor to use in determining what grade to select is the stain you plan to use. Imperfections are less noticeable with darker stains.

LAMINATE PRODUCTS

When your creative side tells you to install wood but your practical side knows it just won't hold up to your kid's antics, a wood-floor lookalike may be just the thing. Faux wood laminate floors provide you with the look you want but temper it with physical wear and care properties that accommodate kids well. Laminate is particularly suited to children's bedrooms and playrooms where stain- and scratch-resistance and easy cleanup count. In fact, manufacturers offer warranties against staining, scratching, cracking, and peeling for up to 15 years. To clean it, just run the vacuum over it or use a damp mop. You never have to wax it.

The installation of laminate flooring is reasonably a quick and relatively easy do-it-yourself project. You can apply it over virtually any subflooring surface, including wood and concrete. It can also be applied on top of an existing ceramic tile, vinyl tile, or vinyl or other sheet flooring. It even works over certain types of carpeting, but check the manufacturer's guidelines before doing so.

VINYL AND OTHER RESILIENT FLOORING

Price, durability, and easy maintenance make resilient flooring an attractive and popular choice for a kid's room. Do-it-yourself installation, an option even for those who are not particularly skilled or experienced, can mean further savings.

Resilient flooring comes in sheets or as tiles and in an enormous array of colors and patterns. With tiles, you can combine color and pattern in limitless ways. Even the sheet form of resilient flooring can be customized with the use of inlay strips, but that's not a do-it-yourself job.

Cushioned sheet vinyl offers the most resilience. It provides excellent stain-resistance; it's comfortable and quiet underfoot; and it's easy to maintain, with the especially attractive no-wax and never-wax finishes that are often available.

CARPETING AND RUGS

Carpeting offers an enormous variety of material, style, color, pattern, texture, and cost options. Wool carpeting is the most durable and the most expensive; it also has the advantage of being naturally fire-resistant. Carpeting made from synthetic fibers offers the greatest variety in terms of color, pattern, and texture; in the short run, it's certainly more affordable. A good compromise would be a wool-synthetic blend, offering a reasonably wide variety of design options, plus some enhanced durability without an expensive pure-wool price tag.

During the manufacturing process, carpet fibers can be woven, tufted, needlepunched, or flocked. Tufted carpet comes in one of three styles: *cut pile* (suitable for use in any room); *loop pile* (very durable, especially in high-traffic areas); and *cut-and-loop pile* (multicolor types are excellent at hiding soil). In general, woven carpet is the most durable; flocked carpet is the least durable.

Wall-to-wall carpeting provides a soft, warm surface for a baby to crawl on. To keep maintenance at a minimum, buy carpeting that has been treated for stain resistance.

The type of fiber, the density and height of the pile, and the thickness and quality of the yarn are other factors that will affect the good looks and life span of a carpet, as will the padding that is installed underneath. They will all affect the price tag, as well.

Area rugs are an excellent device for creating separate play and sleep areas within the room or for dividing the space for sharing. They're also a relatively inexpensive way to add accent colors that help to tie the overall scheme together. However, area rugs should always be backed with a nonskid material. You can hold down small rugs by attaching a hook-and-loop strip to the rug and the floor.

Carpeting and rugs are easy to maintain — vacuum cleaning is all that's required for regular upkeep. Because kids can be tough on any flooring, protect your carpet investment by buying one that is treated at the mill for stain resistance. A periodic cleaning with a steam or shampoo machine will keep most good-quality carpets fresh through years of use.

Smart Tip

CARPET-STAIN REMOVAL. Kids will be kids, and so accidents will happen. The cardinal rule for removing a stain from carpeting is to always clean up a spot or spill immediately, using white cloths or paper towels. Blot, never rub or scrub, a stain. Work from the outer edge in toward the center of the spot, and then follow up with clean water to remove any residue of the stain. Blot up any moisture remaining from the cleanup by layering white paper towels over the spot and weighing them down with a heavy object.

▶ To remove a water-soluble stain, blot as much of it as possible with white paper towels that have been dampened with cold water. If necessary, mix a solution of $1/4$ teaspoon of clear, mild, nonbleach laundry detergent with 32 ounces of water, and then spray it lightly onto the spot. Blot it repeatedly with white paper towels. Rinse it with a spray of clean water; then blot it dry.

▶ To treat soils made by urine or vomit, mix equal parts of white vinegar and water, and blot it onto the spot with white paper towels; then clean with detergent solution.

▶ To remove an oil-based stain, blot as much of it as you can; then apply a nonflammable spot remover made specifically for grease, oil, or tar to a clean, white paper towel. Don't apply the remover directly to the carpet, or you may damage the backing. Blot the stain with the treated towel. Wear rubber gloves to protect your hands. Use this method for stains caused by crayons, cosmetics, ink, paint, and shoe polish.

▶ For spots made by cola, chocolate, or blood, apply a solution of 1 tablespoon of ammonia and 1 cup of water to the stain; then go over it with the detergent solution. Do not use ammonia on a wool carpet. Try an acid stain remover—lemon juice or white vinegar diluted with water.

▶ To remove chewing gum or candle wax, try freezing the spot with ice cubes, and then gently scrape off the gum or wax with a blunt object. Follow this with a vacuuming. If this doesn't work, apply a commercial gum remover to the area, following the manufacturer's directions.

A simple rag rug next to this bed underscores the room's country décor and provides a soft surface over the nubby, rough-textured carpet.

CHAPTER 5

The Nursery— Baby's First Room

When it comes to decorating baby's first room, most expectant parents take an interest. Even people who are normally not inclined to care about such matters as curtains and wallpaper want everything to be perfect for their new arrival, right down to the color of the pillowcases. But baby is too young to notice the pink ruffle on the crib skirt or the painted bunnies on the wall. To an infant, the nursery is just a place for sleeping, feeding, and playing with toys in the crib or on the floor. That doesn't mean there shouldn't be ruffles or painted bunnies in the room. By all means, make the nursery as you would like it, even if baby isn't old enough to appreciate all of your efforts. Besides, this is probably the only time you'll be able to impose your preferences on your child's room without objections from the peanut gallery. Soon, he will take an increasing role in these decisions.

One other thing that you have on your side is the luxury of time. While you are waiting for the baby to arrive, comparison shop for big-ticket items. Get started on some of the work, such as painting and installing wallpaper, which you can do at your leisure. If you're on a tight budget, investigate wholesalers and discounters who may be able to save you money, or wait for certain

From quilts to bassinets and cribs, each new acquisition will bring with it all the excitement of new parenthood. With practical and safety considerations addressed, each piece of furniture will become a family treasure.

The repeated use of the same fabric on the crib and in the changing area ties them together visually.

Getting Started

items to go on sale. Just make sure that if you order something, it can be delivered on time. A cradle or a bassinet in your room next to your own bed is fine for a while, and perhaps even convenient, but you'll need a sturdy crib and a separate nursery sooner than you think.

During this time, talk to other parents of newborns. They may have good advice to share about products. You can also research ratings for the safety, easy use, and durability of specific items through organizations, such as the National Safety Council and the Juvenile Products Manufacturers' Association. (Addresses and phone numbers are listed in the back of the book.) Another excellent source of information is the Internet. Most manufacturers have Web sites, as do the aforementioned organizations, that offer special tips about shopping and detailed information about their various products.

Just because you have time, don't squander it. You still have to paint or wallpaper the space, perhaps install new flooring and a window treatment, and furnish the room. Sometimes just thinking about what needs to be done can paralyze you. But don't let it. Here's what to do.

 ONE: Pick a location for the nursery. It can be a spare room or a large corner in a room shared by another young child, if necessary. The latter should be a temporary arrangement. An infant will require your attention often, sometimes during the night, and this will disturb your older child's sleep. Ideally, the nursery should be away from the public areas of the house where there's a lot of activity. Don't choose a room that's next to the home office, where there's noise from computers, printers, telephones, and fax machines.

TWO: **Make a list of projects and tasks.** It could contain everything from adding a room onto the house to simply painting or just buying furniture. If the room needs construction or major renovating, obtain contractors' bids immediately. The earlier you can get the work done, the better. Lots of new materials, such as carpeting and wood products — even some paint — contain noxious chemicals that take time to dissipate in the air. The last thing you want is to expose your newborn's lungs to these fumes.

THREE: **Review your budget.** Decide how much you can afford to spend. Buy what you really need first. Skip the cute accessories until you've purchased the necessities.

FOUR: **Decide on a look with staying power.** Will it be something old-fashioned, newfangled, plain or fancy, inspired by a favorite nursery rhyme or bedtime story? Narrow down the field, and then look for furnishings to reinforce your ideas. It's wise to stick with a motif that you can retain through the toddler years at least. That way you won't have to redecorate before your child is school age. If you want to include Babar or Barney, for example, do it with a pillow or some other accessory that can be changed when it becomes too babyish for your maturing boy or girl.

A painted nursery-rhyme theme decorates various walls and surfaces in the nursery on these two pages. Otherwise, the furnishings were kept simple.

Design Decisions

Every nursery must serve a number of functions. Primarily it must provide a temperate, safe sleeping area for the baby. A changing and dressing station is also essential. The nursery must accommodate a comfortable rocker, glider, or chair and side table with a lamp where Mom and Dad can feed or comfort the baby at night. There should be a chest of drawers to store clothing, but a nursery with room left over might also include play space or toy storage. Just keep it simple. Don't crowd the nursery; just fill it with the essentials and leave enough space on the floor so that there is room for baby to explore, crawl, and play.

Most of the time, furniture arranging is a matter of common sense. Furnishings will fit into the room in a finite number of configurations, but not all of them are pleasing or practical. Begin by placing the crib. It is likely the largest piece of furniture the room will contain, and it requires some safety planning. Keep the crib away from windows to avoid drafts and any risk posed by an open window. If one side of the crib will rest against a wall, keep the area free of wall hangings. Also, make sure the crib is a safe distance from any heating and cooling vent or radiator.

The changing table should be near the door, if possible. That makes it easy to pop in with baby when necessary. But clean clothes and diapers should be within reach.

Plan a changing area carefully. Make sure to include an easy-to-reach location for clean clothes, diapers, and other necessities that will allow you to keep your hands and eyes on the baby.

Smart Tip

ESSENTIAL NURSERY FURNISHINGS CHECKLIST. The nursery calls for basic furniture for the baby's basic needs. Fill in later with those things that you discover will make it easier and more comfortable for you to care for your child.

- ☑ Crib
- ☑ Changing Table
- ☑ Chest of Drawers
- ☑ Comfortable Chair or Rocker
- ☑ Side Table
- ☑ General Lighting
- ☑ Flooring
- ☑ Table Lamp
- ☑ Mobile
- ☑ Baby Monitor

Shop for a crib that meets the standards of organizations such as the National Safety Council or the Juvenile Products Manufacturers' Association.

NURSERY FURNISHINGS

You don't need a lot of furniture in a nursery, but there are a few items that should be part of your plan: a sturdy crib, a changing table, a rocker or a glider, a chest of drawers, a side table, and a lamp. A clothing armoire and a toy chest are optional. All of these items come in any style from country to contemporary. Should you try to match the nursery's style to the rest of the house? Doing so makes for a cohesive look, but it isn't a mandate that you have to obey. Do what you want. Even if your home is sleek and modern, the nursery can be slightly more traditional to make it more cozy.

The Crib. If you have to choose where to save a few dollars and where to splurge, invest your money in a good, solid crib. One thing to think about if you're considering a crib that converts to a junior bed (also called a "youth bed") is that you may be using the same mattress; so the sleeping surface really doesn't get any bigger. Besides, by that time, your now potty-training toddler will be delighted to have a real big boy's bed to go with his new independence. If you decide to go with a convertible crib, make sure the mattress is twin-size.

An antique crib, left, is charming—but it may not meet recommended safety standards. Guardrails on this changing table, below, protect an infant from rolling onto the floor.

The Consumer Product Safety Commission has set forth standards with which all new cribs must comply. If you're reusing an older crib, it may not meet those standards. If the crib is an antique, you may want to reconsider with a reproduction. It's a good idea to check any crib for safety. Is there any part of the crib, the corner posts for example, that can snag clothing or cause choking? Are there cracks in the finish? Is there a cutout design that could catch baby's arm or neck? Are the rails spaced $2^3/8$ inches apart or less? Does the mattress fill in snugly around the walls of the crib? You should not be able to fit two fingers between the mattress and the side of the crib.

A crib should be adjustable to three or four different mattress heights to accommodate baby as she grows. Also, it has to be solid. Give it a good shake to make sure that there are no missing screws or loose joints, slats, or knobs. As the baby gets stronger, she will jump in the crib, so you don't want to risk a collapse. Any crib must be easy to operate. Lift and lower the rails. Try doing this with one hand, because there are times when you'll have to lower the rail while holding the baby with one arm.

The Changing Table. You'll be changing diapers for two to three years, so make sure you buy the right one. Look for a changing table with guardrails and safety straps. You'll also need a place to store diapers, lotion, cloth towels, and clothes within arm's reach. Some changing tables come with shelves underneath, but that means you'll have to bend over to get what you need, which takes your eyes and hands off the baby. A shelf installed on the wall above the table is a better idea. You could use a portable crib on top of a dresser as a changing station as well. When you don't need it anymore, just remove the crib, and the dresser is ready for a hutch or a mirror.

If you can, purchase a changing table that lets the baby face you as you change him; it's a more comfortable position for you and baby. See the illustration on page 78, which shows an example of an efficient changing station for the nursery. The table is the central design element.

A Dresser. Sometimes parents postpone large furniture purchases until a child is little older. In that case, a hand-me-down chest or dresser is fine because you'll still need a place to store the baby's clothes. Just make sure that the finish isn't chipping and that the joints are solid. Pull out the drawers to make sure they don't stick; if so, lubricate the runners. (Refer to "Good Furniture Construction," on page 47 in Chapter 3, for more tips.) If you're buying something new, don't choose anything on face value; sometimes manufacturers cut back, making the face of the drawer deeper than the actual depth of the drawer. Drawers have to be roomy in order to accommodate the storage needs of your child as she grows. Consider this: One sweatshirt of an average-size sixth-grader fits into the same space as a stack of four infant-size clothing items.

A Chair. A nursery really needs a rocker or a glider. Because this is where you'll sit while feeding or just holding the baby, it should be comfortable for your body. Shop for something that will support your lower back. A chair that you use with a newborn will last through childhood into adulthood if it is

well-constructed. Look for one with padded cushions covered in an easy-care, stain-resistant fabric.

Lighting. Recessed or ceiling-mounted can lighting provides even general illumination for any room. Whatever general light source you choose for the nursery, be sure to install it on a dimmer so that you can lower the light level for a sleeping baby. Most people also use a table lamp beside the nursing chair. Another option, one that will prove safer when your baby becomes mobile, is a wall-mounted fixture. Because babies are attracted to light sources, choose ones that will shade baby's eyes from the glare of a bare bulb. And, never install a lamp within baby's reach. (For specific tips on lighting, refer to page 52 in Chapter 3.)

Flooring. The most logical choices, hardwood, laminate, and resilient flooring, are all fine materials for a nursery floor. Children spend a lot of time on the floor and spill all sorts of things on it. Few parents will go out of their way to install a hardwood floor just in a nursery, but should it exist in the room, it's not a bad performer. A polyurethane-sealed wood floor requires minimal care. A simple vacuuming and occasional dust-mopping is all that is needed to keep wood, laminate, or resilient flooring clean. Because they are not unyieldingly hard surfaces, like stone or ceramic tile, they don't pose much danger for those first tentative steps, unless polished to a high-gloss finish. With an area rug that has a nonskid backing, such a floor can be made relatively risk-free and comfortable for playing.

If your budget is tight, you could treat an old wood floor to an artful painted finish. Try stripes or a stenciled pattern. Another money-saving creative solution is a painted canvas floorcloth. All you need is a pattern, easy-to-work-with acrylic paints, a stencil brush, and disposable foam brushes. You can find these materials and instructions at any craft store.

A pretty carpet anchors this room. Using a nonskid pad is essential. In some cases, an adhesive backing on the rug will do.

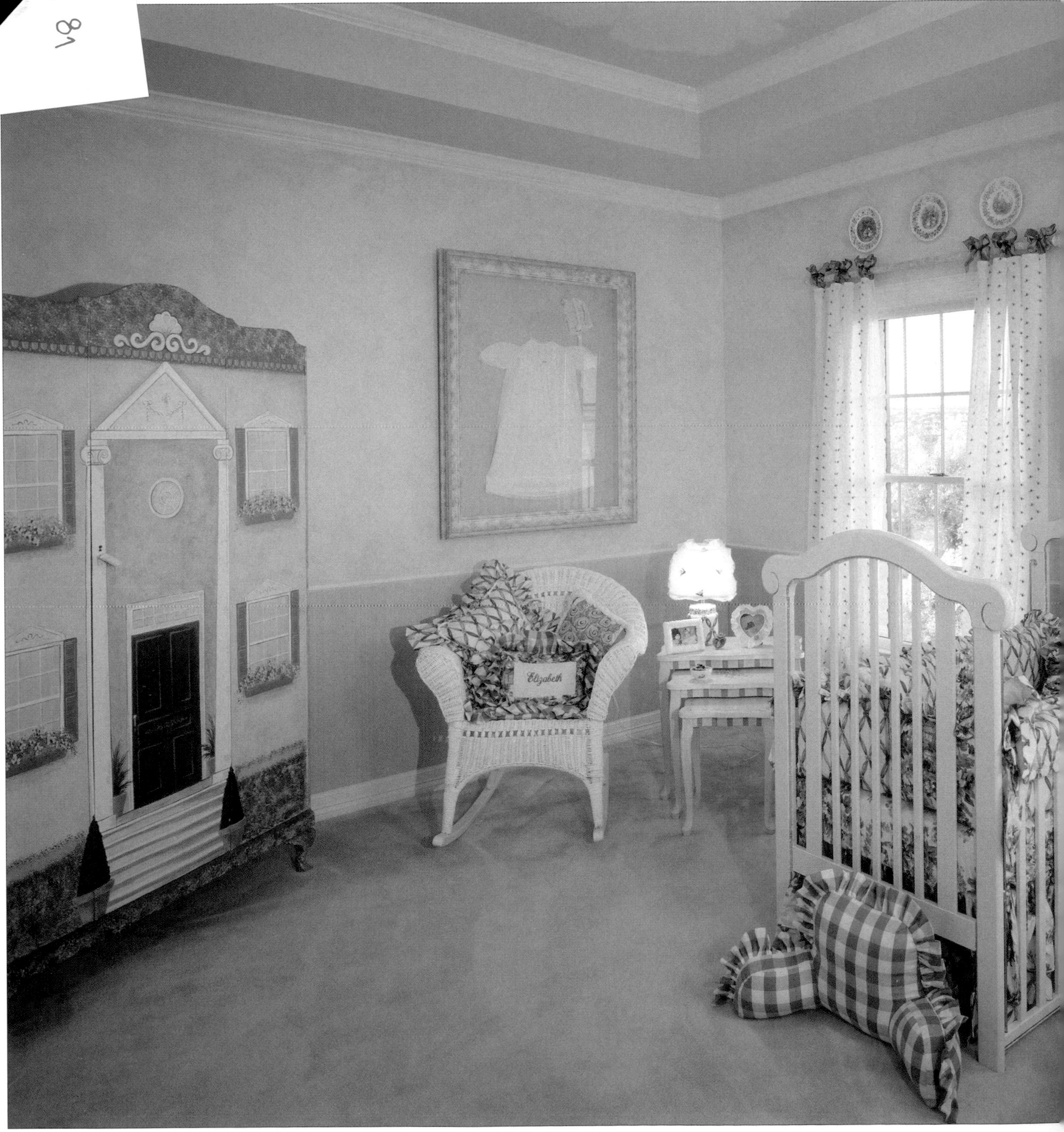
Elizabeth

Carpeting, on the other hand, muffles noise and, especially where drafts are a problem, lends warmth. Falls are naturally cushioned and tentative walkers tend to do well on a carpeted surface. But it can be expensive, especially good-quality wall-to-wall carpeting, and it harbors dust mites and other irritants for the allergy-prone. If you choose carpeting and expect it to last through the years, buy one that is stain-resistant and neutral in color so that your choices for other surfaces aren't limited when you're ready to make a change in the future.

Accessories. Most are optional, but a mobile over the crib and a baby monitor are practically essential. Because newborns are more sensitive to movement than some other visuals, such as color, mobiles are very stimulating, especially ones that play tunes. A reliable baby monitor lets you stay in touch when you're out of the room so that you can hear the baby's noises. When you shop for these items, check to see if they meet the standards of the Juvenile Products Manufacturers Association.

Pretty painted details, left, accessorize this nursery. Above, soft wall art safely dresses up a corner where a newborn's cradle is placed.

Primary colors, above, look cheerful in this room. Soft, muted shades, right, have a peaceful quality. Although you might have a preference, your baby won't notice the color scheme very much.

Pulling Together a Look

Some parents envision a bright, cheerful place where baby will be stimulated by a variety of bright shapes and forms. Other Moms and Dads have something subtle in mind. Although it is true that a baby's eyesight gradually develops over the first six months of life, it's never too soon to include simple patterns and shapes near the crib and changing table. You can do this with linens, mobiles, and soft wall art that will attract a newborn who has a fairly well-developed sense of touch. Stick to simple geometric shapes that are easier for baby to recognize. While wallpaper, curtains, and other accessories can pull together a look or theme for the room, baby won't really take much notice of these.

As mentioned in Chapter 2, color is really up to you. Although some child-development experts believe that sharp contrasts, such as the pairing of black and white, stimulate newborns, they also acknowledge that primary colors (red, blue, and yellow) are recognized by babies in the early months, as well. Yet another study suggests that babies stare longest at yellow, white, pink, and red. None of this information is conclusive. And there is no evidence to suggest that a particular color is harmful. Follow your own instincts.

THEME DECORATING

A common device used in children's rooms is theme decorating. This involves repeating one motif throughout the room. It can be anything from a simple graphic to a fairy tale to a cartoon or nursery-rhyme character. It's really an easy way out if you're stumped for ideas or time. You can find wallpapers and borders, curtains, and linens that feature some popular themes, but be prepared to make changes once your little one develops a mind of his own. Painted murals are another way to do this, often uniquely. But, unless you're a skilled artist, you'll have to hire professional help, and that can be considerably more costly than hanging wallpaper. Still, the effect may be worth the expenditure.

On the other hand, you don't have to decorate with a theme. Some of the most beautiful, classic nursery designs rely simply on traditional decorating elements and a pleasing interplay of color, pattern, and texture. Frankly, if you want to get longevity out of your design, this is the way to go.

THEME ALTERNATIVES

Approach the room as you would any bedroom. That will make it easier to incorporate the interests of your toddler later. Floral, plaid, and geometric designs can all work as harmoniously in a baby's room as in any other bedroom. You can give the room a formal air with lace window dressings or a cozy, casual feeling with rich flannel-checked accessories. Besides, if you keep things simple, you can add a wallpaper border or a bed set that picks up on a motif that your child chooses on her own once she's old enough.

Gender-Neutral Design. It's all about preference. Yes, you can use flowers in a boy's room or a jungle theme in a girl's room. As for color, research shows that women's favorite colors are nearly identical to men's. So where did this custom of pink for girls and blue for boys come from? Look at it this way: You can be an iconoclast, a traditionalist, or you can avoid the conflict altogether by keeping to a gender-neutral theme.

There are lots of colors and motifs that are not gender-specific; stick to them if you're in doubt. Gingham checks, stripes, plaids, and solids in bright, lively colors will work better than floral prints. As decorating motifs, the sun, moon, and stars are a safe choice, and although space exploration and solar system designs used to carry boyish overtones, with heroes like Sally

Sidestep the gender issue by decorating your baby's nursery with a scheme that isn't explicitly boyish or girl-like.

Whatever theme you decide on, take care to make your nursery
a cheerful, safe environment for your child.

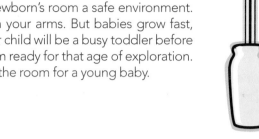

SAFETY IN THE NURSERY. It's not difficult to make your newborn's room a safe environment. After all, a baby spends most of its time in the crib or in your arms. But babies grow fast, becoming more independent with each day. Because your child will be a busy toddler before you know it, you may want to think ahead and get the room ready for that age of exploration. Otherwise, here's a checklist that will help you child-proof the room for a young baby.

▶ Install outlet caps and covers on all electrical outlets.

▶ Play it safe with electrical cords. Don't run them under the carpet, and don't let them dangle from a tabletop or dresser.

▶ Use only blinds and shades without looped cords.

▶ Your baby's ability to pull herself up on the crib rails will likely coincide with her teething schedule. To protect her from swallowing paint or varnish chips, install snap-on crib rail protectors.

▶ Install child-proof locks on drawers and cabinets.

▶ Tack down carpets.

▶ Keep the crib far enough away from any window so that the baby can't grab any cords or curtains or try to climb out the window.

▶ Remove small objects and toys with small parts that baby might swallow.

▶ Make sure furniture is assembled properly.

▶ Hang a mobile out of the reach of baby. Once baby can stand, remove the mobile.

▶ Keep the side rails up at all times when baby is in the crib.

▶ Install a smoke alarm in the room.

▶ Use a monitor to listen to the baby when you're away from the room.

▶ Follow the recommendations of the Consumer Product Safety Commission regarding cribs.

Ride to look up to, it's a perfectly appropriate motif for any child's room. Baby animals are equally associated with either gender, but hearts will imply "girl." Nursery rhymes and fairy tales are good choices, especially if both a boy and girl are the main characters — as in Hansel and Gretel or Jack and Jill. That's one way to be safe from gender stereotyping.

FINISHING TOUCHES

After the wallpapering and painting is finished, the curtains are up, and the furniture is placed, comes the time to give the room its finishing touches. If you've exhausted your budget, don't worry: You can accessorize charmingly with the baby's belongings. Who hasn't smiled with delight at the sight of cute little baby shoes and those tiny little first outfits? Hang them in full view from a Shaker-style pegged rack. Display charming baby quilts or blankets that you received as gifts simply by draping them over the chair. Use inexpensive but pretty ribbon as a tieback to dress up plain curtains, or glue it to the edges of a plain lampshade.

Precut stencils, stamps, and blocks, which are available at craft stores, let you customize everything in the room from furniture to fabric. Materials are inexpensive and come with easy directions. Just keep the stencil flat against the surface you are decorating and offload excess paint. You need a separate brush for each color you use; blot paint into cut-out areas, don't brush it on. Be sure to clean the stencil between applications.

Stamps or blocks with raised patterns are even easier to use than stencils — just load them with paint, blot off excess paint, and then press the stamp or block onto the surface.

A fanciful pegged plaque is both a useful and decorative accessory.

HOW TO CREATE A PAINTED SKY EFFECT

One of the softest, prettiest looks you can create in a nursery for either a boy or a girl is that of a peaceful painted sky. This is one painted effect you don't have to be a skilled artist to render. All that it costs is a little bit of your time (a weekend) and some flat blue and white latex paint. You simply apply it over a base coat of warm-white latex paint. (If the ceiling is already painted white, your base coat is already done.) Follow these steps.

You Will Need

Flat white and flat blue latex paint	4-inch-wide decorator brush
Paint tray and buckets	2-inch-wide decorator brush
Mixing sticks	Bucket of clean water
Roller	Clean rags
	Gloves

1 Once the base coat dries, apply the blue sky paint with a brush or roller. Let it dry. Then working at a 45-degree angle, slap white paint over the surface using short, random strokes from a 4-inch-wide decorator brush, as shown. Pull the paint out until it's thin in some areas, and overlay it in others so that you create an uneven color overall.

2 If you wish, imitate the color gradation found in the sky by leaving the tops of walls and the centers of ceilings more blue. Work the paint so that it has a mottled effect. This mottling begins to suggest where you should place the clouds.

3 Use a dry 2-inch-wide decorator brush tipped with the white paint to establish cloud shapes in the light sections. Use random, flowing strokes, as shown, to smooth and blend the two colors. Be loose, and create billowy shapes.

4 The final finish: To complete the finish, mix 8 parts water with 1 part white paint to make a thin wash. Brush this wash over the entire surface, and then let it dry. It has a softening effect that breaks up the blue and pulls everything together.

Toddler to age 5
Room to Grow

A toddler, even a very young one, forms an attachment to his room and understands it clearly to be his own. He knows his clothes belong in the room, his toys live there, and every night it is where he comes to sleep. It's also likely the only room in the house where he is allowed to touch most of what he sees. So it's important to plan a room that not only pleases your child's senses but also serves his needs. This is a period of transition, from totally dependent baby to ever-more independent tot. It's the time for moving from crib to bed, for acquiring possessions, and for developing play skills. So in addition to the decorative elements you choose for the room, there are several other important factors that should be part of your game plan: buying a bed, determining storage needs, planning play space, and making the room safe.

By the age of 2, your child will demonstrate numerous likes and dislikes. You may be able to discern some of her preferences for specific colors and theme subjects by the toys she gets most excited about or particular articles of clothing she likes more than others. Although it's too early to assume that these favorites will last, you can use them as clues to help you design a room that reflects her personality and stimulates her imagination.

This transition bedroom for a small child includes areas for sleeping and play. The young resident has already made the move to a grown-up bed, and enjoys a large area for active play. A tepee is available for imaginative entertainment, as well as a traditional rocking chair for those times when a story is just the thing needed before settling down for the night.

If *Baa, Baa Black Sheep* collapses him into a giggle fit every time he hears it, you could key your design off that rhyme. It might be the inspiration for a wall mural, for example. Perhaps you can bring to life a favorite storybook, the one he insists you read at least a dozen times a day. Maybe your toddler's fascination with trucks, trains, dolls, or animals can inspire a theme. Think of this decorating project as a way to delight your little one. With your knowledge of what sparks his interest, you can make it just right.

Also, as you pull together a motif or decorative details, keep to things that you can change with ease and relatively little cost, particularly if you plan to use the room for the next child who will have her own personality. Replacing curtains and linens and

Divide the room into zones for sleeping, playing, and studying. Here, there's ample floor space for play and a table and chairs for tea parties and crafts. A desk, right, awaits the future student.

adding a fresh coat or two of paint are quick pick-me-ups for a room; new wallpaper and rugs are a bit more expensive, but not major undertakings. If you're planning on a painted mural, a motif that can be modified to suit the next child is a good idea. For example, if a Tarzan theme was perfect for Johnny, but a bit too wild for Jane, bring back the artist to add colorful bows to some of the animals. In other words, create a flexible design that can serve whatever interests your child. Don't get caught up in passing fancies; use accessories and details when you want to update the scheme periodically.

Getting Started

The transition from nursery to a big boy's room can be a little disruptive for a toddler, even with his growing sense of independence. To counter any fears brought on by the change, gradually get your child used to the idea. Here's what you can do to prepare your youngster for the changes.

ONE: Communicate. It's never too soon to start talking to your child. Explain that this is her room. Parents of toddler-age children have heard the word "mine" often enough to know that the promise of "ownership" is enticing.

TWO: Involve your child. Let your tot "help" you by bringing some of his things into the room, for example. Show him where his toys and clothes will go and ask him to put them away.

THREE: Appeal to her pride. Emphasize that because she's not a baby anymore, she's going to sleep in a grownup bed now, and she'll have "big girl" furniture.

A Room Plan

Room to play is probably the most important thing you can provide. Kids of this active age need rocking horses and indoor gym sets. If space permits, divide the room into separate zones for sleeping, storytelling, making crafts, and playing. This might help you to contain some of the mess if, for instance, finger paints are permitted only at the crafts table (where snacks may be taken, too) and toys must remain in the play zone. You can visually partition the space by using different flooring types, such as carpeting near the bed, wood or a wood-laminate in the play zone, resilient or vinyl flooring in the craft area.

Tight on space? Arrange all the furniture against the walls to free up floor space for playing in the center of the room. Look around and decide what you don't have to keep in the room. If floor space is at a premium, don't include a chair and side table in the plan for the time being. (You can sit next to your child in bed when you read to him.)

Capture your tot's imagination. Here are three creative, playful motifs for a child's room. From the left, a jungle, a cabbage patch, and a beach retreat.

Smart Tip

ESSENTIAL FURNISHINGS CHECKLIST. Start with these basics to get started. You don't have to buy everything on the list, but it will serve as a guideline for planning your budget.

- ✓ Bed
- ✓ Chest of Drawers
- ✓ Toy Box
- ✓ Nightstand
- ✓ Lighting
- ✓ Small Table and Chairs
- ✓ Flooring

By this time, your youngster's toy collection is also threatening to overcome every room in the house. A toy box, shelves, baskets, and bins, especially ones on wheels, can contain the clutter. You can even encourage habits of neatness at this age by teaching your toddler to put things away.

FURNISHINGS

If your crib converts to a toddler bed, you're pretty set, as the nursery dresser will likely suffice for the time being, as well. However, as discussed in Chapter 3, "Furnishing Your Child's Room," it's probably a better idea to buy an adult-size bed at this stage. With the addition of a child's table and chair set and toy storage, these items may be able to carry you through until your youngster is 5 or 6 years old.

The Bed. A twin-size adult bed is ideal, although you may have to buy a double bed somewhere down the line, as your child gets older and wants to have friends for sleepovers. Why not a toddler bed? First, it may not have guard rails, although it is lower to the floor. Plus, a toddler bed is seldom constructed with box springs, which means it cannot provide the proper support your child needs. (For advice on shopping for a

Storage and display space can be equally contained within the shelves of a full-size armoire, but be on the lookout for child-size furniture pieces such as this wicker chaise longue.

This sleigh bed is of a style that makes it suitable for children and adults alike. Pushed against the wall—and with minimal other furniture in the room—it leaves plenty of floor space for playing. The basket is an easy catchall for toys.

children's rooms, and a large mirror that can shatter is a potential disaster. Install one later when you feel your child is ready.

If you are considering more furniture at this time, clean-lined designs that work with a variety of decorating styles are best. Beds with built-in storage are particularly practical. Furniture that is designed specifically for kids, and has met the standards set forth by the Juvenile Products Manufacturers Association and the Consumer Products Safety Commission, can be considered risk-free. But if you're looking at furniture designed for adults, take into consideration any design elements that may present choking hazards or ornate woodwork that can cause injury by catching little arms and legs.

What's more important is storage for all of the toys that start to accumulate at this age. When your tot gets tired of something, put it away in the attic, garage, or basement for a while and bring something else out.

mattress, refer to page 38 in Chapter 3.) For a young toddler who is adjusting to a grownup bed, there are twin beds that come with guard rails that can be removed later.

If you don't want to commit to a specific furniture style now, simply buy the twin-size frame, mattress, and box spring. A headboard and a foot board are optional, and can be added later if you wish. Otherwise, something improvised, such as a stenciled design on the wall behind the bed, can be changed easily and is a good idea.

Well-constructed novelty beds can serve well, and may be passed from one child to the next. Although some youngsters may want a bed that's not childlike in a couple of years, novelty beds remain popular with most children until age 8 or 10.

Storage. Probably one dresser is still sufficient for a child this young. You can be the judge. Pass on the dresser mirror for the time being, or just put it in storage. Things tend to fly across young

Buy an unfinished piece of furniture and decorate it with paint. This small armoire keeps the clutter behind closed doors.

Crates, cubbies, and plastic bins provide excellent toy storage. Kids get out of bed at night, and they can trip over objects left on the floor. Bins on wheels are handy for picking up at the end of the day. A traditional toy box is useful, but make sure it operates with safety hinges. If you want to use an old trunk or one that wasn't intended for toys, that's fine, as long as you retrofit it with safety hinges.

Shelves are always a good idea. If your child is a climber, a low shelf is an invitation to explore, and it may be dangerous. On the other hand, if you keep shelves low enough on the wall for your child to reach, you're helping her to pick up after herself. Adjustable shelves that rest on supports attached to wall-mounted steel brackets offer the most flexibility. Otherwise, plastic crates that can be used as cubbyholes may be affixed to the walls for storage. Anything heavy that can fall over, such as

Organization is the secret to keeping any kid's room neat. Attractive cubbies, left, house buckets of tiny toys. A recycled changing table, below left, has shelves that hold games and books. A wire-coated closet system, below, handles extra clothes.

tall bookcases or other tall storage compartments, should be bolted to the walls as well.

For bulkier items, install a closet organizer. Easy-to-assemble wire-coated systems come in numerous configurations and include bins, baskets, drawers, and shelves. Lower hanging rods make it possible for kids to hang their clothing, as do children's clothes trees and pegged racks.

There is another option: custom-built storage, which will serve your child's needs for years to come. It's a good investment, particularly in a small room that defies organization. If you hire a professional carpenter, explain that you expect the pieces to accommodate your child's storage needs now (stuffed animals, storybooks, toys) and in the future (heavy textbooks, stereo equipment, and perhaps a TV). Don't forget to get references and check them out. Then obtain several estimates for the work.

Small Table and Chairs. A tot-sized table and chair set provides a place for fantasy and creativity. Little ones like to get their fingers into things, and so this is where they can safely play with paints, crayons, clay, and other messy things. It can be a spot for light snacks and teddy bear tea parties, too. Sturdy plastic sets can take a real beating, and they can be scrubbed down without causing harm. You can buy a set made of wood, too, or look for an unfinished table and chairs that you can customize with paints. (See pages 98–99 for an easy technique.)

Lighting. Lighting needs change as children grow. At this stage, good general lighting spread evenly around the room is necessary, as well a soft night light that can be left on for the many times you may have to check on or tend to your little one. You'll need a reading light for storybook time, too. It can be near the bed or next to a chair, wherever you'll sit while reading. Task lighting for toddler-age children isn't necessary. Shorter attention spans and a lack of coordination make long-term concentration on one task rare at this time.

For good general lighting, install recessed or ceiling-mounted lamps with a dimmer switch. A table lamp can be risky because it can be knocked down when small children become rambunctious. And running kids can trip on cords. Instead, use a wall-mounted fixture with a light source you can direct. Never put a lamp where a youngster can reach up and get injured by a

This ceiling-mounted fixture is attached to a dimmer switch, which allows the parents to control the light level—bright for playing, soft for settling down at night.

hot bulb. (For specific tips, see "Lamps and Other Lighting Fixtures," on page 52 of Chapter 3.)

Flooring. Just as in a nursery, flooring for a toddler's room should be chosen with practicality in mind. Little ones spend a lot of time playing on the floor, and they spill stuff. You need a surface that can stand up to toys that are dragged from one end of the place to the other, and that can be swept and mopped up easily. That makes resilient flooring or a laminate product the most suitable. Wood, especially if it has been sealed with polyurethane, is easy to keep clean, although it may scratch, depending on the finish. If you want it to stay looking good, invest in a finish that can be damp mopped. For warmth underfoot near the bed, install an area rug with a skid-proof backing. Something you can pop into the washing machine makes sense, unless the area rug is large. In that case, regular vacuuming will take care if it.

Carpeting is another option, but one that may be better suited to an older child's room because it's not as easy to keep clean as other types of flooring. It may also pose a problem for children with allergies and asthma because it can harbor dust and other allergens, making regular daily vacuuming a must.

Decorating for Toddlers

Themes carried over from the nursery are still suitable for children in this age category. Depending on your nursery choices, you may not need to change the wall and floor treatments at all. Babyish themes will become inappropriate by the end of the toddler stage, but some may last well into the first couple of years or until school age.

If you're starting from scratch, a good place to begin is with color. At this stage, asking your child to choose a favorite is futile. He may give you an answer, but it's likely to change every time you ask. Studies, a bit more reliable than those conducted with

babies, indicate that bright colors attract toddler-age children. Red and yellow, in particular, are stand-out favorites. In general, bright colors stimulate psychologically, while cool colors have a relaxing effect. You may want to experiment with the effect of various colors on your child. Try out a lively scheme if you think your child could use more stimulation in his development. Conversely, see what happens to your overly energetic tot when he's in a room of quiet, soft colors.

Pastel colors appear to be less appealing to toddlers than bright ones, but that doesn't mean you have to replace them if they already exist in the room. If you can easily make a change with a wallpaper border or new curtains, for example, that's great. But you're not going to do any harm by sticking with what you have. If you decide to make changes, go with geometric prints,

All it takes is imagination. "Spots" cut out of black construction paper were applied to the windows, left, to underscore a dalmatian theme. Cardboard stars and a campfire, above, pull together a "night out under the open skies." A kid-size tent and picnic set take the place of standard furniture.

stripes, plaids, or any other motif that isn't too youthful and the wallcoverings, curtains, and bed linens will last well into the school years or until your child is tired of them.

Because young children are more attracted by color than form, color is an excellent way to get your child excited about a new room. If you dislike bright or primary colors, choose a neutral overall scheme and accent it with bright red, blue, or yellow, or a combination. So many toys and accessories designed for children of this age are decorated in these colors, and that will make accessorizing the room easy. Another approach is to experiment with various tints and shades of one primary color to find attractive variations on a monochromatic (one-color) scheme. For example, try using different shades of blue for the walls, trim, window treatment, and bed linens. If you get tired of this later, just change the color of one of these elements.

TWO OR MORE TO A ROOM

At this age, it's not unusual for two children to share a room. If the co-occupants are nearly the same age, the arrangement is

Decals, stickers, stencils, and prepasted wall borders often feature juvenile themes. Use them to easily perk up plain white walls. They're all easy to replace or paint over when you want to make a change.

fairly easy. Each child should have a separate bed. An activity table can be shared as well as the play space. It's a good idea to provide separate toy storage for each youngster, but this can be as simple as assigning one toy box or shelf to each child. A bedside table at this age is not necessary, but it always comes in handy—even if it's just for a night light. For a symmetrical look, one shared table between twin beds is fine. Chairs or futons that convert to twin beds are another space-saving option, but bunk beds are not recommended for children under six years old.

A situation where a school-age child must share a room with a much younger brother or sister is more difficult, but sometimes unavoidable. For one thing, both children need their own separate area in the room. Plus, you have to provide storage for the older child that the toddler cannot access for his own safety. Share with your older child the job of seeing that dangerous items are kept out of reach. However, the safety of a younger child is too much responsibility for any kid.

Avoid a decorating theme that is too youthful. Keep the motif neutral by avoiding wallpaper and fabrics with childish themes. Pick something that would be appropriate for any age, such as a floral print in a room shared by girls or plaid for a boys' room. Perhaps paint the walls a solid color instead. You can use accessories, such as a night light, soft wall art, and a few stuffed animals for the younger child's half of the room; then let your older child hang posters or prints on her side of the space.

Furniture that divides up the room is a good idea if there is enough space to allow for modular pieces. Otherwise, a folding screen will allow privacy for your older child. If necessary, it can be folded up during the day to allow light from windows on one side to spill into the entire room.

You can also divide the room in half visually by choosing two different themes. For example, if it's a boys' room, decorate with a baseball theme on one side and a hockey theme on the other side. Two themes for two girls could be dance and gymnastics. Or you could decorate with two totally different motifs as selected by each child. Use complementary color schemes to unify the two areas while providing visual separation. Anything you can do to make sure each child feels comfortable is helpful.

FINISHING TOUCHES

Refrain from adding too many accessories to a young child's room, especially if that includes delicate or small objects. The point is to make the space a free zone, where everything is touchable and safe. For example, because lower parts of walls traditionally take a beating from toddlers armed with crayons, chalk, and markers, why fight it? Instead, mask off a section and paint it with chalkboard paint. This is a latex product that you can paint over later when you're ready to change the room again. Using chalk, little kids can draw and practice writing their ABCs to their hearts' delight. Plus, their scrawls and scribbles will be erasable, so they can create new ones over and over. Chalkboard paint can also be used to create a tabletop drawing surface or to decorate doors.

Another way to pack the room with personality is with decorative paint effects. Sponged-on or ragged finishes let you add something extra to ordinary painted walls, and the dabbed-on texture camouflages smudge marks and greasy little fingerprints. The walls can be painted over when the child is older and it is time to freshen and update the look of the room.

Displaying personal items that belong to your child brings something of her personality into her room. Left, a child-size clothes tree, vanity table, and chair identify who lives in this room.

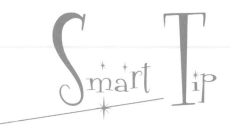

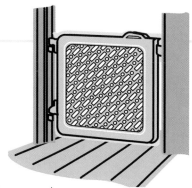

SAFETY IN THE TODDLER'S ROOM. Toddlers seem to have a sixth sense that draws them like magnets to a potential source of harm. It's really just their natural curiosity and growing independence. Here's a list of things you can do to keep them free from harm.

▶ Install caps and covers on all electrical outlets.

▶ Use window guards that restrict the size of and access through window openings.

▶ Tie or wrap up long cords on blinds and shades so that they have no loops and are out of reach.

▶ Use molded plastic electrical cord covers.

▶ Install devices in place of your switch-plate covers that lower the switch to a child's level.

▶ Remove lamps completely unless they are safely out of reach.

▶ Secure heavy furniture to the wall with bolts or with straps and brackets.

▶ Keep toys off the floor at night.

▶ Use small slide locks placed out of reach to prevent opening and closing of bifold doors that can catch fingers.

▶ Keep conventional doors from closing with foam doorstops that fit over the top of the door.

▶ Use one-piece doorjambs to eliminate the choking hazard posed by ordinary doorjambs that have removable parts. Install doorknobs without locks.

▶ Use bed rails.

▶ Don't place furniture directly under a window.

▶ Use a toy chest with safety hinges.

▶ Don't put a toy on top of a high shelf or dresser. Make the toy accessible if it's going to be in view.

▶ Discard anything with small parts.

HOW TO CUSTOMIZE UNFINISHED KID-SIZE FURNITURE

Treat an unfinished wooden table and chairs and a toy chest to a creative paint finish. It's easy!

TABLE AND CHAIRS

Sand the table and chairs, and then wipe them with a tack cloth. You can use the suggested colors or your own choices. Apply one or more coats of primer, and let it dry. Then follow with two coats of light blue paint for the base. Let it dry.

Mix the neutral glaze with medium-blue glaze until you get the desired shade. Apply an uneven coat of tinted glaze to the table and chairs, including the legs (Step 1). The green glaze that's applied to three of the chair's back spindles can be made by adding some of the yellow paint to the blue glaze mixture.

While the glaze is still wet, use the paint comb to create the patterns (Step 2). On the tabletop, work it in a wavy motion. On the chair seat, work it vertically, and then go over it again horizontally to make a checked pattern. On the flat back panel of the chair, comb alternating blocks of vertical and horizontal strokes. Let the glaze dry thoroughly. It's best to wait overnight before proceeding with the next step.

 You Will Need

Child's unpainted wooden table and chairs	Multipurpose primer
Acrylic craft paint in light blue, yellow, black, and brown	Flat foam paintbrushes
	Sponges: natural
Decorator glaze in neutral and medium blue	Masking or painter's tape
	Craft knife
Animal cutouts	Mixing container
Decoupage medium	Paper towels
Rubber multipurpose paint comb	Soft lint-free cloths
	Chalk pencil
Stencil brushes	Ruler or straightedge
Spray adhesive	Sharp-pointed scissors
Sandpaper	Sealer
Tack cloth	

1. Apply glaze over the dry base coat. On large surfaces, work one small section at a time because you will have to apply the technique while the glaze is still wet.

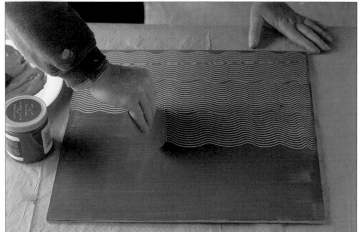

2. Hold the comb at an 80-degree angle, and drag it through the wet glaze toward you. Apply pressure to the comb so that it blends slightly and cuts through the glaze as you pull it toward you. Make curved or straight lines, but keep strokes smooth and steady. Try to avoid stopping in the middle of a stroke.

Project continued on next page ▶

3 Arrange cut-out animal motifs from wallpaper or wrapping paper around the table and chairs, marking their placement with the chalk pencil; then apply them with decoupage medium. Add the words "Two by Two" with black and brown paints. Apply two coats of sealer to both pieces.

Paint Combs

Paint combs are used to create lines by dragging the instrument through wet paint or glaze. You can purchase plastic or metal paint combs (pictured) from a craft store. If your project is small, improvise by using a 4-inch-wide stiff piece of cardboard. To create tines, notch one length of the cardboard with a zigzag pattern. If the cardboard comb gets soggy, stop working with it and make a new one.

TOY CHEST

Sand the chest, and wipe it with a tack cloth. Apply two coats of primer, let it dry, and then follow with two coats of off-white paint. Let it dry. As with the table and chairs, you can use the suggested paint colors or your own.

You Will Need

Unfinished pine blanket chest	Sandpaper and tack cloth
Latex paint in off-white	Multipurpose primer
Acrylic craft paint in true blue, light brown, and pale gray	Flat foam paintbrushes
Acrylic gloss paint in green-blue	One cellulose sponge for each brick color
Upholstery foam, 3 inches thick	Masking or painter's tape
Fabric	Craft knife
Decorative trim	Paper towels
Fabric glue	Chalk pencil
Sharp serrated knife	Ruler or straightedge
Staple gun	Scissors
	Sealer

Measure each side of the chest, and divide the panels to establish a grid for sponge-block print with a small space between each block. A lot depends on the size of your sponge; you may need to cut the sponge to fit. Mark the placement of the sponge blocks on the sides of the chest with a chalk pencil and a straightedge, leaving about a $1/4$-inch space between each one. Because the blocks don't have to be perfectly aligned, use your eye to establish the spacing between each one.

Use a separate paper-plate palette and sponge for each color of paint. Wet each sponge with water and wring out the excess moisture. Press the sponge into the paint, and then offload some of the paint onto paper towels to avoid paint drips and runs. Firmly press the sponge onto the surface to make a clear impression (Step 1). Do the same with each alternating color, leaving about $1/4$ inch of space between each imprint (Step 2). Wipe drips with a damp sponge while the paint is still wet. Reload each sponge with paint; blot it before every application. Just in case your grid isn't perfect, start at the center; then continue to the right and left. That way, if your calculations come up a bit short, you can cheat on the size of the blocks at the end of the row. When it's dry, apply two coats of sealer.

Press a sponge that has been loaded with paint, and blotted, firmly onto the chest's surface to make a clear impression.

The blocks do not have to look crisp and perfect. In fact, unevenness in the application of the paint and slightly wobbly edges will simply add charm and texture to the overall effect. Unlike a faux finish that should be as realistic as possible, creating a pattern of blocks or bricks with a sponge is a technique that is intended to look hand painted.

THE CUSHION

To make the cushion, take a piece of fabric that's large enough to cover upholstery foam cut to fit the top of the chest. Position the foam on the top of the chest lid. Fold the fabric over the foam to the back side of the chest top. Work from the center out toward the sides, smoothing wrinkles in the fabric and keeping the pattern straight, and staple it onto the lid. Miter the fabric at the corners of the chest top. Finish by gluing your choice of decorative trim along the edge of the chest top.

The final effect demonstrates consecutive rows of blocks in alternating colors. Leave a 1/4-inch space between each block. You can create straight rows of blocks or reproduce the stagger of a real brick pattern.

The Early Years— Widening Horizons

As a child enters the primary grades, his needs shift again. In the bedroom, play space is still a requirement, but a place for doing homework and projects materializes as an equally important element. Besides play and work areas, additional sleeping accommodations for overnight guests become considerations. These are key acquisition years—more toys, more clothes, sports and hobby equipment, a stereo, CDs, a television, a phone, a computer, a printer, electronic games. Kids are great collectors. There are all sorts of bric-a-brac and whatnots that attracts them. You name it: If it's out there, it will eventually wind up in their room. If you haven't instituted an anti-clutter plan yet, now is the time to get children into a routine of putting their things away.

A well-planned room is crucial at this age because it must fulfill so many needs: play, work, storage, sleep, and the entertainment of friends. Of course, these needs develop gradually over time. But it's better to think ahead than to try to retrofit something into the design later. That doesn't mean you have to give your six-year-old her own phone, but you might want to think about where you could install a phone jack later, especially when it's time to hook up a computer. Furniture earmarked to house future electronic purchases can be used to contain a doll collection or large stuffed animals for now.

Invest in good-quality furnishings that will be adaptable as your child grows. This bed's appeal is good for several years, and even the bed-curtains can be retained with a change of fabric for the Roman shades.

A fresh twist on the nautical. Classic bunk beds, painted a bright, glossy white, leave room for a kid-size sitting area with floor space left over for play. Stars are sprinkled around as a design motif, and a "porthole" mirror adds to the look.

Getting Started

Your child is now old enough to be involved in some of the decorating process. Depending on his personality and interests, by the primary grades, he can participate in decorating decisions, such as color choices and furniture styles. Of course, what he may not understand is that certain things are passing fads, and he may tire of them sooner than he realizes. Although it may be hard to convince him, you can offer compromising solutions to any fad-inspired or unusual requests.

Most kids have lots of ideas to offer. Listen to them. Write them down. If she can't be specific about what she likes, show her pictures in magazines. Talk to her about her friends' rooms. Find out what she likes or doesn't like about her existing bedroom. Avoid leading questions, such as, "Wouldn't a border of hearts and flowers look pretty in your room?" The idea is to find out what pleases your child, not to coax her into pleasing you. To get a dialogue going with your child about what she might like for the room's décor, follow these steps.

SMART STEPS

ONE: Talk about color. The makers of children's toys and clothing know how to pick colors that kids, especially, and their parents will like. There are always the traditional favorites, but if you browse through the kids' clothing department in a store, you will notice certain color trends, which typically reflect those of the adult world. Ask your youngster to pick out the colors that he likes. Make a note of them. Try this again in a few days to see if he's consistent in his selections. If so, you've got a color to work with. If it's something that's too trendy or unconventional for your taste, use it as an accent color or for accessories, such as the curtains or bed linens. That way, you can please your child, and change the items when they become tiresome.

TWO: Discuss themes or patterns. She may be too young yet to think in these terms, so ask your daughter to tell you what kind of room she would like. If she says she'd like it to look like her old-fashioned dollhouse, maybe a Victorian theme is the way to go. If she says she'd like it to look like outer space, perhaps a sun, moon, and stars theme is in order. In other words, use these clues to direct your choices for some of the room's elements, such as a wallpaper pattern or a style of furniture. You might even be able to show her various options.

The seaside theme is continued in the floor design. "By the sea, by the sea, by the beautiful sea" forms a stenciled border. A painted three-dimensional star decorates the central space in front of the bunk beds.

Take home samples from the wallpaper or fabric store that you can look at together.

THREE: Make a list of things that will go into the room. Besides the obvious—a bed, a chest of drawers—there are other furnishings and items that you and your youngster may want to keep in the room. If it will be something large, such as a fish tank, you'll have to account for it in your floor plan. A hobby table, storage for arts and crafts, a ballet bar, a train set, or other space-consuming items must be measured and accounted for, but you can veto some things that may be better stored elsewhere. For example, sports equipment should go in the garage, and a noisy nocturnal hamster may be kept in a cage in the family room or the playroom.

FOUR: Narrow down the field. You can't leave it all to a child, no matter how much you want to encourage creativity and participation. Some choices are just too sophisticated for a kid to make. Mixing patterns and even some color schemes should be guided by a mature eye. When it comes to selecting

A room divided: Floor-to-ceiling sliding panels compartmentalize the different areas for playing, studying, and sleeping in this inventive arrangement for a large suite shared by two children.

furniture, a major investment, allow your better judgment to take over with regard to size, durability, versatility, and affordability. It's a lot easier to change a quilt or a bedspread than it is to replace furniture.

A Room Plan

At this point it's a good idea to refer back to Chapter 1 to review the section entitled "Evaluating the Space," which begins on page 13. If you haven't already fully furnished the room, you'll have to do it now. Drawing up a floor plan will let you work

with different layouts until you find the best one for the space. Experiment with a new room arrangement that reflects your child's needs at this time. If you are adding a computer to the room, locate it where the screen will not reflect light from a nearby window (or plan to install the proper adjustable window treatment). Remember, the glare from natural or even an artificial light source can cause eyestrain. Apply forethought to mirror placement as well as locating the television screen. Glass reflects light. For optimum TV viewing, the distance between the monitor and the seating (typically, the bed) opposite it should be three times the size of the screen. Make sure to note electrical outlets on your plan as well.

Making a drawing of the space will also help you judge the suitability of various pieces of furniture with regard to scale and proportion. As your child matures, he'll have increasing needs for storage and display. He may want a larger bed, a place to study, and so forth. This is how the room can get crowded. Modular pieces are a good idea, as is under-bed storage in the form of built-in drawers or ones that can be purchased separately and come with wheels for easy access. When floor space is tight, additional closed or open storage can be created with shelves. Bins, baskets, and boxes can keep things that you don't want on display out of sight. Converting an old toy chest into storage for all those bulky items, such as sweaters, extra quilts and blankets, and out-of-season clothing is a smart idea,

too. Re-paint or cover it with leftover wallpaper to coordinate with the rest of the room's décor.

While it's true that today's American children are taller than their ancestors were at the same age, kids are still shorter than the average adult. Keep that in mind when you're hanging a mirror or planning storage. If she can't reach the hanging rod in the closet, she is not going to put away her clothes. Make it easier for her—and you—by installing a rod within her reach. See the illustration on page 115, which shows you how to design a closet for your school-age child.

FURNISHINGS

Furnishings that help to organize the room will keep your stress level down, while adding to the overall livability of the space and comfort of your child. Multifunctional furniture may solve the problem of addressing all of your child's lifestyle needs in one room. The key is to know specifically what those needs are.

Smart Tip

ESSENTIAL FURNISHINGS CHECKLIST. More clothes and toys, books, homework papers, awards, collections, and hobbies will require more furniture storage for your school-age child. Here's a checklist of basic furniture necessities.

- ☑ Bed
- ☑ One or more freestanding or built-in chests of drawers
- ☑ A freestanding desk or a built-in desk or desk shelf (30 inches high)
- ☑ Shelving
- ☑ Nightstand
- ☑ Lighting
- ☑ Flooring

Furnished simply with the basics—a bed, two night tables, and a desk with shelves—this child's room is comfortable yet not "overdone." The old trunk and large basket are decorative as well as practical for storage.

Every child is different. Some kids don't want their own computer; they're fine using the one in the family room. Even a desk can be optional if your kids do their homework at the kitchen table (and you like it that way). Eliminating some items leaves space for a dressing table, perhaps, or an armoire for a TV or clothing spillover if the room's closet is small. So, just as you would analyze your own needs when furnishing other rooms in the house, do this with regard to each child's room before furnishing it. Also, refer back to Chapter 3, "Furnishing Your Child's Room," which begins on page 36, for specific tips about furniture quality and shopping.

The Bed. Remember, at this age your child's universe begins to broaden, and he is starting to develop friendships. That means, soon he may want a friend to spend the night sometimes. So it's not a bad idea to plan for sleepovers when you're deciding on the type of bed to buy. Bunk beds are one way to go. Other options include a bed with a trundle or a double bed. If there's enough space in the room for a love seat or chair that opens into a sleeper, either one offers another solution. If all you can manage is a simple twin-size bed, relax: Kids are adaptable.

They love an excuse—such as having friends to sleep over—for camping out on the floor either in a sleeping bag or just with an extra blanket and pillow for the night.

Storage. Probably you'll need more than one dresser or chest of drawers, so this may be the right time to get rid of the hand-me-down furniture. Because most parents only want to buy furniture once, items that will adequately serve your child's needs, hopefully, through the teen and possibly the college years are the most practical. Avoid styles that are juvenile or saccharine. A little girl who likes white painted furniture with ribbons and bows will hate it when she's a "sophisticated" 15-year-old. Leave the cute stuff to the accessories unless you're willing to replace the furniture later.

To suitably store clothes for your growing child, choose a double- or triple-width dresser. The latter is usually a combination of drawers and behind-door storage. Style doesn't matter; it's better to buy something that will fit in the space that you have. Don't forget to take measurements of the room and compare them to the specifications for each piece of furniture

A furniture option adaptable for sleepovers, this trundle bed, below, provides ready accommodations for a guest but remains neatly tucked away until needed. Small cabinets with shelves, right, offer a child accessible storage for small objects.

A good lighting scheme includes three types: here, ambient light from a wall lamp, task light at the bedside, and decorative light on the walls above the headboards. The whimsical neon fixtures are fun as well as useful as night lights.

that you may be buying. Never make assumptions about size. Measure everything because so-called standard sizes can vary from one manufacturer to the next. If you can, purchase a chest (generally, just a taller set of drawers), especially one with deep drawers that can hold bulkier items, such as heavy sweatshirts and sweaters or an extra blanket.

An armoire is a versatile piece that can be outfitted to hold TV and stereo equipment, a computer and all of the related accoutrements, or it can be equipped with shelves or a hanging bar. As an investment, it's worth its cost many times over because, with modest retrofitting, you can use it repeatedly in different ways and in almost any room in the house.

A night table next to the bed can hold a lamp and an alarm clock. One table on each side isn't necessary if you don't have the space, but plan for at least one. It can also be a small chest, a small covered table, or even a storage cube.

Although a desk is optional, it does provide a place for a computer and for keeping schoolwork, books, and some hobby materials organized. School-age children accumulate tons of paperwork, and you may want to save some of it. Consider spray-painting a two-drawer office file cabinet. A bulletin board can hold artwork or favorite photos. (See instructions on pages 118–119 for making an upholstered collectibles board.)

Don't forget to include some kind of shelving to hold collected items, trophies, books, or to create some attractive display space for it. Always make sure that shelves are well anchored and cannot topple over. If the unit is freestanding, put heavier items on the bottom shelves, and bolt the unit to the wall.

Lighting. Proper lighting becomes more important, especially ambient and task lighting. The traditional irony is that a good lighting scheme is seldom noticed while bad or insufficient lighting is recognized instantly. Aside from eliminating eyestrain, good lighting complements your decorating efforts. It makes colors ring true, and it makes people feel better, too.

Besides general (ambient) lighting, such as a ceiling-mounted fixture or recessed ceiling canisters, plan to keep a light next to

One table lamp serves two nicely. In this room furnished with twin-size beds, a central lamp meets lighting needs at bedside for the resident child as well as a guest.

the bed. When reading in bed, your child will be lower to the mattress than an adult. Therefore, adjustable lamps with articulated arms that can be positioned to meet a child's changing needs as he grows are wise choices.

Include good task lighting at the desk. Ideally, the bottom of the lampshade should stand about 15 inches above the work surface. The shade itself should measure 16 inches wide at the bottom, 14 inches wide at the top, and have a depth of 10 to 12 inches. Place the lamp on the right side of the work surface if your child is left-handed or to the left if she is right-handed.

Collections and awards displayed on shelves can be illuminated, too. If you will be installing built-in furniture, such as a wall system, it can be equipped with light. Or consider installing recessed fixtures or strip lights that can be focused on a particular object or area. See "Lamps and Other Lighting Fixtures," on page 52 of Chapter 3 for more advice.

Flooring. To create a cohesive scheme, choose a flooring material that will complement the room's décor. Wood, either natural or a laminate-product look-alike, will work well with country, traditional, or period furnishings. An area rug, anchored with a nonskid mat, can underscore the look and add comfort without compromising safety. A hooked, braided, or rag rug has particular appeal in a country setting. If you choose a busy print for the wallpaper or curtains, pull out a solid accent color from the pattern and select a matching solid-color rug or mini-print rug. If other surfaces are plain, you may want to liven up the room with a bold pattern underfoot.

Wall-to-wall carpeting complements contemporary designs, but it is appropriate for any style décor. To reinforce a modern theme, pick a geometric pattern or a solid color. There are also styles to coordinate with traditional furnishings. An Oriental carpet or one with a floral print is a good choice that coordinates with traditional rooms. For more information on various options for flooring, see page 69 in Chapter 4.

Accessories. A doll collection, trophies, snow globes, wind-up toys, action figures, ceramics, miniatures, or any objects of fascination are details that bring something of your child's personality into the room. This is a great time to start a collection with your child. What to collect? It can be funny hats, unusual flea-market finds, ceramic figurines, special posters or prints—anything that captures his or her imagination. Create a display on walls and shelves. Let your child create his own art or frame his favorite comic strips. If wall space is at a premium, install shelves above the window frames; this makes the display a part of the window treatment.

A well-organized closet not only makes getting dressed easier but also provides the basis for teaching the child to be orderly and to begin to take responsibility for caring for his own wardrobe and personal possessions.

Decorating

Regardless of what kind of wallpaper you might think would look nice on the walls, from this point on, your child will want to add her opinion to the discussion. Don't worry too much about formal decorating. Your child, in her own way, will add her personality to the space. Posters, activity schedules, and her framed artwork will take the place of the baby quilt and nursery-age pictures and accessories that you chose for her the last time around. To keep thumbtack marks and tape marks to a minimum, look for lightweight acrylic frames to display her best paintings and drawings. This type of frame will make it easy to change the artwork and update the collection with new ones as your child desires.

An artful arrangement of the child's beloved dolls or "life-long" collection of favorite footwear may be the answer to display and storage if you're looking for a way to add some personal interest to an empty space in the room.

As soon as your child begins sports, dance, music, or some other hobby or activity, there will be trophies, ribbons, and certificates to display these honors. Shelves are perfect for storage or collectibles, but for this purpose, too. A large cork-board is great for pictures of friends, stickers, memos, and school-achievement certificates. If you want to make it special, cover the cork surface with leftover wallpaper. To eliminate the need for tacks and pushpins, wrap the board with cotton batting; then cover it with fabric. Use ribbon or fabric tape to create a trellis pattern. Then you can simply tuck pictures or cards inside the ribbon. You can upholster an area on a wall or a folding screen this way to create a larger display as well. See the next page for easy step-by-step instructions.

FINISHING TOUCHES

By now, you have a good idea of who your child is, and what his likes are. This should help you to find a theme that can pull the entire room together. Sometimes something as simple as a wallpaper border can do it for you. Luckily, many manufac- turers make themed borders that illustrate motifs that are popular with this age group. They include everything from dancing to sports, and they are easy to put up or take down when you or your child is ready for a change.

Another thing that you can do to carry a theme through is to cover a cornice for the window treatment with fabric that, like wallpaper border, comes in an assortment of juvenile themes.

Decorating with personal objects is a good way to give your child some hands-on input in the room's décor. The collectibles board over the bed is an easy wall-decoration project adaptable for any age.

You can even coordinate it with the border or wallpaper pattern. Although the cornice is a semi-permanent window treatment, its covering can be altered or changed as your child's interests and tastes mature. At first, you can install the cornice alone or over a fabric roller shade for a simple, understated look. Later, to update the room without replacing the cornice fabric, replace the shade with shutters or curtains for a fresh change of appearance.

Smart Tip

SAFETY IN THE YOUNG CHILD'S ROOM. Even though your school-age youngster has progressed beyond the baby stage, you should take these measures to make his room safe.

▶ Install a smoke alarm above the door.

▶ Put away toys and keep the floor clear at night so that children who get up to use the bathroom don't trip.

▶ Install a cool-to-the-touch night light.

▶ Don't run electrical cords under rugs. Keep them tucked away behind furniture to prevent a tripping hazard. Never use any electrical device with a torn or frayed cord.

▶ Use anti-skid mats under area rugs. Make sure carpeting is securely tacked down.

▶ Attach bookcases and shelves securely to walls. Store heavy items on bottom shelves.

▶ Don't use glass-topped furniture.

▶ Make sure the bedroom door cannot be locked.

HOW TO MAKE AN UPHOLSTERED COLLECTIBLES BOARD

You can make a pretty place to display anything from postcards to report cards in just a few easy steps. You don't need special skills or tools, and all it takes is a few minutes to a few hours (depending on the size of the surface you plan to cover). You might enlist the help of your child. Older children may want to make a collectibles board on their own.

You can use a corkboard or a foam board, which should be available at an art-supply store. You can adapt the project to the surface of a folding screen, a wall, or a closet door. Skill-wise, all that's important is that you take accurate measurements. The only tools you'll need are a measuring tape, scissors, and a staple gun. Fabric that's been leftover from another project, such as curtains, a dust ruffle, pillows, or cushions, will do fine. However, you can use sheeting or scraps from the fabric store. If you use a multi-color print, pick out the ribbon or fabric tape color from one of the hues in the fabric. If the fabric is a solid, choose a contrasting color or, in the case of ribbon, a print.

Start by measuring the board. You'll need a piece of cotton batting and a piece of fabric that is large enough to cover the front of the board plus a few extra inches to wrap around all four sides. Attach the cotton batting to the back of the board with staples (Step 1). Miter the corners for a neat finished appearance. Do the same with the fabric. Then cut enough strips of ribbon or fabric tape to create your pattern. To make the pattern featured here, start with vertical rows of ribbon strips (Step 2), followed by horizontal rows, and then finish with a diamond pattern (Step 3). Attach the strips with upholstery tacks or sew-on buttons. Tuck pictures underneath the ribbon strips.

You Will Need

Measuring tape	Coordinated ribbon or fabric tape
Scissors	
Corkboard (or similar surface)	Upholstery tacks or buttons
Cotton batting	Staple gun
Fabric	

1 Measure the board. Cut a piece of cotton batting that is large enough to cover the front of the board and wrap around all four sides. Turn the board over, and staple the batting to the back. Then cover the batting with a piece of fabric, attaching it the same way. For a neat look, miter the corners.

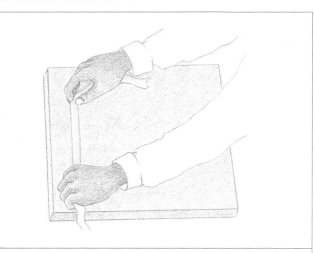

2 In this example, the pattern is rather complex and comprises a series of vertical, then horizontal rows of ribbon followed by a diamond configuration. Measure and cut lengths of ribbon; the number will depend on the size of your board. Attach each one to the board with upholstery tacks.

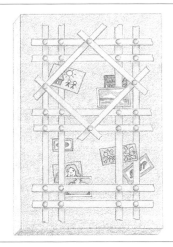

3 The finished board. Tuck pictures, postcards, award certificates, and so on underneath the ribbons. That way, you don't have to worry about pushpins or tacks. If you don't want to use upholstery tacks to hold the ribbons in place, substitute sew-on buttons for them.

Alternative Ribbon Patterns

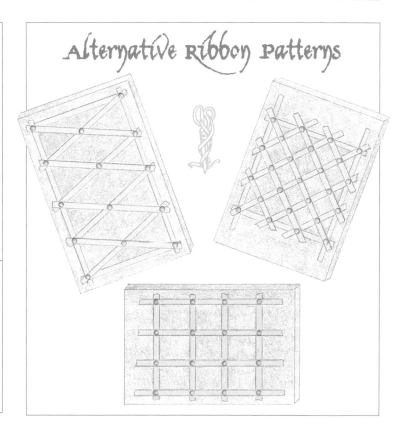

CHAPTER 8

Teens' Rooms— Their Self-Expression, Your Standards

It's only a matter of time until your maturing child lets you know that he's outgrown his kiddy room. At this stage, you are not so much decorating a room *for* him as you are doing it *with* him. In fact, renovating the room may be entirely his idea. Most likely, he will have definite changes he wants to make, and you'll have to accommodate his preferences, as well as his lifestyle needs, which are increasingly more grown-up. Toys and other embarrassing reminders of young childhood are out. Teenagers require more storage for clothing, an expanding music collection and electronic equipment, a personal grooming spot, a place to do increasing amounts of homework, as well as an environment that they can consider private and totally their own.

Decorating a room for an older child can be challenging, but it can be accomplished without too much stress — especially if you remain open-minded and don't try to impose all of your ideas on the project. Just as she is developing her own personal style regarding matters such as clothing, books, music, and so forth, she is finding her way in the decorating world, with ideas that may be unlike your own. There will be mistakes, but remember when she took her first wobbly steps? You didn't criticize her if she stumbled then, so don't do it now.

Tailored to the teen's personality, this room reflects the freewheeling decorating and furnishing choices of its young owner. Note that the jazzy colors and prints are confined to linens and accessories that can be replaced easily. Allowing her to express her own preferences, within your budget, assists her on her way to becoming a confident young adult.

This snug alcove contains cozy sitting or sleeping space, a number of shelves for treasured items, and a built-in display board for special mementos.

Of course, as a parent, you can set ground rules and disallow anything you feel is really outrageous or beyond your means. And who knows? Your teenager may show you a thing or two about creativity during the process.

Color is one area that is sometimes a source of contention between parents and children — particularly when a teenager chooses an unconventional or particularly intense color scheme. If it's something that you think is too unusual or strong for the walls, suggest a compromise, such as bringing in the color with accessories or as an accent.

At this age, boys as well as girls want a room that reflects their individuality and independence. Boys may or may not be as interested in the style of the curtains as the girls, but they know what they don't like. Even if your teenage son says he doesn't care about the wallpaper pattern, don't assume he's going to be happy with something you think is appropriate. If he doesn't want to get very involved in the project, fine. But pick out some samples of fabrics, wallpaper, and paint chips and show them to him. That way you can eliminate anything he doesn't like *before* you make the changes.

Aside from decorating issues, teenage boys and girls have things in common in terms of room requirements. First, they want privacy. Unlike the days when they sat and watched TV in the family room or did their homework at the kitchen table while you prepared dinner, they spend most of their time in their rooms. There's no need to be alarmed. Your son or daughter isn't withdrawing, just growing up. Besides, they should have a place to study or talk with friends without the distractions of the rest of household. Today, that often means designing a sociable space with an efficient workstation that is equipped with a computer and a printer, proper seating, as well as storage for CD-ROMs, and other supplies.

Most teens also want their own phone line (and answering machine, possibly), which isn't a bad idea considering how much time they spend tying up *your* phone. The extra line costs a few extra dollars a month, and it can be used for Internet setup as well. That way, while your teen is chatting online, you're not missing important calls.

Don't forget to make room for visiting friends. When kids of this age get together, they want to talk where you can't listen. Again, this is normal. Essentially, it's simply part of the maturation process — kids gradually separating themselves from their parents. Giving them the space, physically and psychologically, is helping them move toward adulthood.

Getting Started

Think of your teenager's bedroom as the precursor to the college dorm room. It's her sleeping space, her study and work niche, her place to entertain, and her private domain where she can talk about boys, hang crazy posters on the wall, and just be alone with her thoughts and dreams if she wants to. If it's comfortable, she'll spend a lot of time there rather than in someone else's home.

A built-in vanity topped with plate glass, left, is easy to clean. Shelf storage is tucked behind a mirrored door. Below, a room layout popular with teens—furniture is grouped in a casual arrangement for studying and entertaining.

By all means, encourage your teenager to become involved with the decorating and renovation process. Ask him to stop by the paint store and pick up color chips. Tell her to bring home fabric swatches and wallpaper samples. Follow these steps to get your teenager to take more interest in and responsibility for the project.

 ONE: **Work out a budget together.** Tell him how much you can afford to spend, and then let him decide how to divvy up that amount on individual expenditures. If there's something he wants that your budget can't accommodate, perhaps he can contribute some of his savings or money from a part-time job. Or, instead of paying a contractor to paint the room, suggest to your teenager that if he does the work, the money saved can be spent on something that was off-limits before — the installation of a new phone line, perhaps. Also,

look for less-expensive knockoffs. Very often, you can find a stylish imitator of a pricey accessory, piece of furniture, or material just by shopping around.

TWO: **Let her do the window-shopping.** Magazines, catalogs, and furniture showrooms are good places where she can look for ideas. Tell her to keep notes with the names of patterns, colors, and style numbers, as well as prices. Suggest that she tear out pictures from magazines, and jot down any pertinent product information that might be listed as well. Or hand her a pad of sticky-notes and ask her to tag pages that she likes. You can go over these things with her when you're ready to shop. If there's a decorators' show-house event in your area at the time (usually, around the holidays and in the spring), perhaps you can attend it together to get an idea of what designers are doing.

THREE: **Be the practical one.** Determine the room's measurements, and take along the measuring tape when you go shopping. These are some of the details that he'll regard as tedious and will be happy to leave to you. Draw the line on renovations that not only cost a lot but will require expensive

A cozy window seat adds to the romance of this room. The shelf above the window offers display space. For storage: a bureau—in place of a night table—and a small cabinet.

making over when your teenager leaves for college and you want to use the room for another purpose.

A Room Plan

If you've never evaluated the space in terms of size and shape, do it so that you can maximize its potential. Now that you'll be eliminating a lot of items that your teenager has outgrown, you may be able to improve the room's existing floor plan and furniture placement. If you are purchasing new or additional furnishings, this step is essential. For help, review "Evaluating the Space," on page 13 in Chapter 1.

After years of accumulating lots of stuff, this is a good time to decide what stays, what goes into storage, and what goes into the garbage. Have a yard sale for any toys she doesn't want to save. Use the earnings toward a purchase for the new room. Better yet, donate old toys that are in good condition to a needy shelter, day-care center, or the children's ward of a hospital.

A good way to evaluate the architectural aspects of a room is to empty the space completely. That way you can see its basic

If not, think about ways to accommodate grooming needs in the bedroom. Certainly, a well-lit vanity table and mirror is one solution. Just make sure that there are adequate receptacles for small appliances, such as a hair dryer or a curling iron. A full-length mirror (freestanding or mounted to the back of a door) to check overall appearance and a three-way dresser or vanity mirror to check hair helps. A space-saving lighted makeup mirror that can sit on a shelf or a small, skirted table is an option. Underneath, store cosmetics and small appliances in baskets. Or keep toiletries neatly tucked into pretty hatboxes that can be left on display. Hang a shoe organizer on a hook or inside the closet. Its deep pouches handily store hair accessories, combs and brushes, and small cosmetics. Always include a small wastebasket in the grooming area, too.

If there isn't enough room for a designated grooming area, adding a mirror over a desk can serve the same purpose,

A dresser with a three-paneled mirror is perfect for personal grooming and also visually enlarges the room. Overhead, a pretty collection of hats that can be worn or just admired.

A daybed will grow with a very young teen as she enters adolescence. Its twin-size style adapts for casual seating, right.

bones and check out the condition of the walls, floor, windows, doors, and trim. After years of living, you may notice that some things need a little patching, or more than a coat of fresh paint. Even if all you have to do is install wallpaper and hang new curtains, you'll find that the job goes a lot easier in a room that isn't filled with furniture. When you're ready to put furniture back into the room, try a few sample arrangements on paper first. See the furniture templates in the Appendix.

SETTING ASIDE A PLACE FOR GROOMING

Personal grooming takes on new importance for girls and boys in the teen years. Providing a spot someplace other than in the family bathroom for hairstyling, applying makeup, general primping, and storing toiletries will avoid conflict. If your teenager is lucky enough to have a bathroom of her own, great.

especially if the lighting can be adjusted for the separate tasks. (See "Lamps and Other Lighting Fixtures," on page 52 in Chapter 3.) Reserve one of the desk drawers for grooming aids and mount a hook to the inside wall under the desk in the leg area to hang a blow-dryer. Small storage boxes on top of the desk can hold little items and accessories.

PLANNING A TEEN'S WORK AREA

If you haven't already done so, you're probably going to have to set up a computer station in the room as well. If your son or daughter has been using the family computer until now, and that arrangement is still satisfactory with all parties, fine. If not, and you're ready to take the plunge, don't worry: It doesn't have to look like tech central.

Besides a computer, there is the related equipment. It's unwise to keep electronics on the floor because dust and dirt can damage these items, as can static from a rug or carpeting. So you'll need a desk or flat surface with cubbies or shelves to house everything from a hard drive, printer, monitor, and possibly a scanner to CD-ROMS, floppy disks, and paper. It should be large enough to accommodate a legal-size notepad, as well as a keyboard and monitor. A roll-out tray for the keyboard is a practical option because it places the keyboard at a comfortable height while freeing up room on the desktop. It's important to have a place where papers and items of different sizes can be stored out of sight. Otherwise, you're inviting a mess.

A place for homework with a desk, computer, and other study aids encourages good learning habits. Desks for two teens who share a room can be arranged so that each has a separate space with a monitor and keyboard apiece.

An adjustable chair is essential; a 13-year-old boy will sit taller at 14, and again at 15, and 16, and 17. So make sure the chair is ergonomically sound and offers ample comfort and support for the back of a growing adolescent. And don't overlook proper lighting. Your teenager will need adequate indirect illumination of the work surface. Avoid aiming light directly at the monitor, which will cause glare, or on the desktop, which will produce shadows.

In a room where space is tight, a laptop computer offers a solution. You can link it to a printer elsewhere in the house. Some laptop computers offer wireless (infrared) access to the Internet. Otherwise, your teenager can browse the Web with his laptop simply by plugging it into a phone jack.

You'll also be happy to know that this equipment is increasingly available in versions that take up less space and will fit on a compact surface. For example, there are now flat-panel monitors and scaled-down hard drives that may cost more, but don't require a massive computer station to house them.

If your teenager doesn't want to look at electronic contraptions when they're not in use, no problem. You can house a computer and all of its accoutrements behind closed doors in

Smart Tip

ESSENTIAL FURNISHINGS CHECKLIST. In the teen years, storage needs increase along with the need for extra seating spaces for studying and entertaining friends. Plan for pieces that will do double-duty.

- ☑ Bed
- ☑ Double- or Triple-Width Dresser
- ☑ Tall Chest of Drawers or Armoire
- ☑ Desk
- ☑ Desk Chair
- ☑ Shelving
- ☑ Extra Seating
- ☑ Nightstand
- ☑ Lighting
- ☑ Flooring

either a custom-made or manufactured computer cabinet or armoire. Some of these cabinets come with a drop-down desktop. Just fold it back and close the doors for the look of an orderly room in an instant—every mother's dream.

If two teenagers share a room, you can design a double-length work center with space at each end for a computer, a monitor, and under-desk drawer storage, plus shelving. Both can share the printer and the scanner, if there is one.

Or design a work surface that doesn't have to go up against the wall. That way, each person can sit on either side of the desk. The computer setup can consist of one computer, one printer, two monitors, and two keyboards. Teens can then network for files and games. In a shared work center, each area should also have its own task light and comfortable desk chair as well. Chairs on wheels can be moved around easily.

FURNISHINGS

Sometimes teenagers want to make a complete change in the design or décor of their rooms. Adult furniture is on their list, and if you can afford it, you may go along with this request. But think before you leap into that purchase. In just a few years, when he goes off to college, do you plan to keep the room for his visits home or convert it for another purpose? Will you let him take the furniture when he's ready to move out on his own? How much longer do you plan to actually remain in the house? Can you take the furniture with you if you go?

Specific furniture styles may mean more to your teenager as she is getting a more defined sense of her own style. But sometimes you can re-fashion older furniture by adding a new finish or treating it with one of the decorative paint finishes that are so popular. One new or refurbished piece of furniture can make a big change in the look of the room. See page 135 for easy instructions for adding a new look to an old headboard and chest with paint and paper decoupage. Also, refer back to Chapter 3, "Furnishing Your Child's Room," which begins on page 36, for tips about furniture quality.

The Bed. Because your child has been sleeping in an adult-size bed for years now, consider replacing the mattress and box spring. At best, a mattress will continue to provide adequate

support for about 12 years, but some health experts believe it should be replaced much sooner than that. Certainly, if it's worn, lumpy, or fails to provide a comfortable night's sleep, it should go. See the section called "Beds and Mattresses," which is on page 38 in Chapter 3, for advice about shopping for a quality mattress and box spring.

Even if there's extra seating, your teenager and her friends will flop all over the bed, which becomes a substitute for a couch in a bedroom. Extra throw pillows and bolsters can make this "seating" arrangement more comfortable for everything from watching TV to looking at yearbooks.

Other bedding options that appeal to younger tastes include futons and daybeds. A better-quality *futon* offers enough support for nightly use, but shop and choose carefully. Realistically, it's a good option for extra seating that can be converted easily to an extra bed for friends who want to crash overnight. A *daybed* can double as seating, too, but it has the advantage of a standard twin-size mattress. Many come with a trundle that slides out from under the daybed; some feature a pop-up mechanism that elevates the trundle mattress to the height of a bed mattress.

Storage. Just like adults, teens complain that they never have enough storage. Therefore, it's a good idea to provide as many chests as possible in the room. A double- or triple-width dresser with a large mirror is good for starters. If there's room, include a tall chest of drawers. It's important to have adequate storage for bulky sweaters and sweatshirts, so look for units that have deep drawers to accommodate them.

For extra blankets and pillows or out-of-season clothing, don't give up precious space in the closet. A storage trunk or armoire can easily house these items, as well as serve multipurpose needs. Add a rod to an armoire and you've created a wardrobe; install shelves and use the piece to hold a TV, VCR, or other equipment. A trunk can double as a low table. Plus, you can make use of either of these pieces in other rooms of the house later.

Add stylish sophistication to an older teen's room, opposite, with colorful bed linens and pillows. The pillow's star motif is repeated—hand painted around the ceiling light fixture, inset.

A desk paired with a bookcase provides a work area, below, for a computer and room for projects requiring a flat surface with storage alongside. Supplies are tucked inside containers.

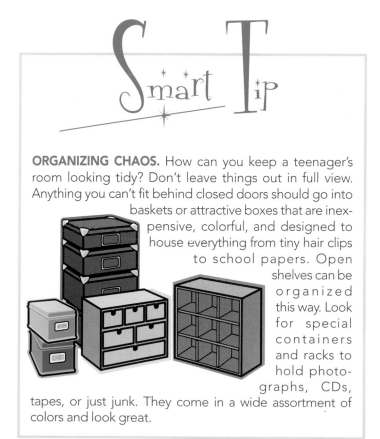

Smart Tip

ORGANIZING CHAOS. How can you keep a teenager's room looking tidy? Don't leave things out in full view. Anything you can't fit behind closed doors should go into baskets or attractive boxes that are inexpensive, colorful, and designed to house everything from tiny hair clips to school papers. Open shelves can be organized this way. Look for special containers and racks to hold photographs, CDs, tapes, or just junk. They come in a wide assortment of colors and look great.

Additional storage pieces can include a lingerie chest, a vanity, and nightstands. But don't forget to make use of every inch of space. The toys that once cluttered the shelves can now hold a sound system, CDs and tapes, speakers, books, collections, and even clothing. Use the space under the bed with drawers on castors that slide in and out easily. Install a closet system. Whether it's custom-designed or a wire rack system that you put in yourself, it will make the closet neater, and easier to find things — it will house a lot more.

In addition to the custom-built computer center mentioned earlier, you have the option of a freestanding desk. If there is a computer and related equipment, look for a desk that is designed specifically for these items. You can find them in various sizes, configurations, and price ranges to suit almost any room. If you're handy with a screwdriver, a ready-to-assemble (RTA) unit is affordable for all budgets. Some desks come with compartments that hide electronic gizmos for anyone who doesn't like the look of high-tech. A small filing cabinet is a must if the desk doesn't come with drawers. A cabinet that is on wheels that can be pushed under the desktop is convenient, but check the clearance first.

Seating. In addition to a desk chair, additional seating is a consideration if there's room to accommodate it. A sturdy upholstered chair, loveseat, or chaise longue, accompanied by a floor lamp, is good for reading or studying. Beanbag or butterfly chairs offer appealing young styling.

Lighting. Good general and task lighting are essential ingredients in the room's design. Add accent lighting to illuminate framed prints, a collection on a shelf, or sports awards. A ceiling fixture or recessed canister lights provide efficient general illumination. Wall sconces and illuminated cove lighting are just two indirect solutions that are highly effective in a bedroom. In a large bedroom, consider spacing recessed fixtures about 8 feet apart for even lighting. An adjustable-arm or gooseneck desk lamp is fine at the desk. For a dressing table or mirrored dresser, use wall sconces or table lamps at both ends to create even, shadow-free illumination for grooming.

An important thing to remember when choosing a lamp is that any flat, reflective surface can be the source of indirect glare, which causes eyestrain. Surfaces that are prone to indirect glare include shiny desktops, mirrors, glass-top surfaces, as well as TV screens and computer monitors. The solution is to aim the light source away from these surfaces.

Flooring. Don't overlook flooring and the role it plays in tying all of the room's surfaces together. Color and pattern choices depend largely on the rest of the room, but a light, neutral scheme offers the most versatility; flooring is a semipermanent element that shouldn't have to be replaced every time you change the color of the walls or the bedding.

In large rooms, an area rug over wood or resilient flooring material adds warmth and coziness. Wall-to-wall carpeting, especially in a light solid color, visually expands the size of the room. It also has another advantage over most other types of flooring — it muffles sound. If you're looking for a way to cut down on the noise, this could be the answer.

Invest in quality storage pieces that either the child can take with him in the future or you can use later in another room. Above, a pine bureau complements a rich plaid wallcovering.

Choose furniture with dual uses. A comfortable chaise longue, opposite, is a good choice for extra seating for guests as well as a place for reading, studying, or napping.

You can't count on teenagers to be cautious about spills and spatters on the floor, so it's always a good idea to shop for materials that can stand up to the abuse kids of all ages can cause. Wood, laminate, and resilient flooring are easy to maintain and clean. Carpeting requires vacuuming and immediate attention when something is spilled on it. For more information on types and care, see the section in Chapter 4 called "Flooring," on page 69.

Decorating

This is really your teenager's project. The styles, colors, patterns, and accessories she chooses will reflect her point of view, but you can offer guidance. Most teens seem to prefer informal furnishings punctuated by casual fabrics such as denim or cotton prints. For color inspiration, take a look at teen fashion. If their clothing has a retro-Seventies look, home fashions

aimed at this market will reflect it in terms of color and motif. Accessories from duvet covers to lampshades and picture frames will carry out the theme.

FINISHING TOUCHES

Your teenager's taste and sense of self may be different at age 17 than it is at age 13, so you'll have to find a way to keep fads and trends limited to items that can be changed without much fuss. Stick to items that aren't permanent or expensive for adding a trendy look, and keep the major elements of the room simple.

A **"curtained vanity" and a shelf** installed on the wall behind the bed, above and opposite, offer decorative storage and display spaces that are both attractive and practical.

SAFETY IN THE TEENAGER'S ROOM. Safety is important at all ages. Go over this list with your teenager, who is old enough to assume more responsibility for her own safety.

▶ Install a smoke alarm above the door.

▶ Keep books and clothing off the floor to avoid creating a tripping hazard, especially during the night.

▶ Don't run electrical cords under rugs. Keep them tucked away behind furniture. Never use a frayed or damaged cord. Don't overload plugs and extension cords.

▶ Install anti-skid mats under area rugs. Make sure carpeting is securely tacked down.

HOW TO TRANSFORM
AN OLD HEADBOARD

Do-it-yourself decorating projects such as the painted-and-decoupaged headboard and painted bedside dresser shown opposite lend a distinctive touch to a room.

Sand the headboard to a smooth surface, wipe it clean, and apply two coats of heavy-duty primer. Let the primer dry; then apply two coats of a light-green satin base paint.

Mask the frame of the headboard. Using a small natural sponge for each color, sponge-paint the center panel with off-white, golden brown, and medium-green paint (Steps 1 and 2).

Cut out three large and two small floral motifs from wallpaper (Step 3). Once the paint has dried, you can mark the placement of the cut-out paper flowers on the headboard with the chalk pencil. Brush decoupage medium onto the back of the cutouts and arrange them in place. Apply a top coat of decoupage medium to the cutouts and smooth out bubbles or wrinkles in the paper. Let it dry. Remove the masking tape from the frame and then mask the center panel of the headboard.

Use dark-green acrylic paint and a pointed brush to create a border of small leaves. Connect the leaves with wavy lines.

You Will Need

Wooden headboard	Fine artist's paintbrushes: #4 liner, medium pointed.
Latex satin paint in light green	One natural sponge for each color paint
Acrylic craft paint in golden brown, medium green, dark green, and off-white	Chalk pencil
Floral wallpaper	Painter's tape
Decoupage medium	Spray adhesive
Gold metallic wax	Craft knife
Sandpaper	Paper towels
Steel wool	Soft lint-free cloths
Tack cloth	Pencil
Heavy-duty primer	Ruler or straightedge
Flat paintbrushes: foam or bristle	Sharp-pointed scissors
	Sealer

1 Load the sponge with a light coat of paint, and then gently dab it onto the surface. Change the direction of the sponge often to avoid a repetitious pattern. Apply additional colors one at a time.

2 Apply consecutive colors to areas that reveal only the base-coat color, but do not obscure it completely. To vary texture, use different-size sponges for each color. Do not apply dense layers of paint, but do overlap and blend the colors.

Project continued on next page ▶

3 Cut out the images you will apply, using sharp pointed scissors that can make clean cuts. With the cut-out motifs in hand, begin to play with an arrangement. To make this easier, mist the reverse side of the image with spray adhesive.

4 The final finish. Check to see whether or not the images appear smooth. Once they are in place, it's important to smooth out air bubbles or wrinkles with your fingertips or a clean foam brush. Don't wait until the decoupage medium dries to do this.

HOW TO PAINT A STRIPED DRESSER

Remove all drawers and hardware. Sand the dresser and drawers and wipe them with a tack cloth. Apply two coats of the primer. Let it dry. Then go over the dresser with the cream paint.

To create the stripes, replace the drawers, and then divide the top and front of the dresser into an odd number of vertical panels. Mark them with a straightedge and a chalk pencil. Each stripe in the example pictured here is approximately 4 inches wide, but yours may be wider or narrower, depending on the overall width of your piece. In the same manner, mark out stripes along the sides of the dresser.

Remove the drawers to make painting easier. Beginning with the center stripe, run a line of masking tape along the outside edges of every other stripe. Smooth down and burnish the edges of the tape with your fingers to secure it in place. Using a wide foam brush, paint the center and every alternate stripe with two or more coats of the light-green satin latex paint. Allow it to dry. Remove the tape, and then mask the alternate stripes in the same manner with new tape. Paint these stripes with a clean foam brush using two or more coats of the cream paint. Let it dry. Remove the masking tape.

To create the trellis design on the front, divide the drawer panels into three sections. The center section should consist of three stripes, with two stripes comprising the sections to the left and

You Will Need

Three-drawer unfinished wood dresser	Fine artist's paintbrushes: flat, liner, pointed, and round in assorted sizes
Latex satin paint in cream and light green	Masking or painter's tape in several different widths
Acrylic craft paint in medium green, red or dark pink	Craft knife
Sandpaper and tack cloth	Paper towels
Steel wool	Chalk pencil
Multipurpose primer	Ruler or straightedge
Flat foam paintbrushes	Sealer

1 It's an excellent idea to practice on a board before attempting to hand paint a design on the actual surface or object you are decorating. After lightly drawing or transferring a traced design onto your surface, allow the brush to do the work. Press down or ease up to vary the thickness of the lines.

right of the center. With a chalk pencil and a straightedge, make a straight line along the outside edges of each center section. Within each section, draw a line from each corner to the opposite one; then make a small "+" in the middle of each section. You'll use all of these lines as guides. Thin the medium-green paint with a small amount of water. Practice hand painting (Step 1). Then create tiny leaves along the first lines that you drew using the pointed brush. Next paint wavy lines along each "X" with a liner brush. Arrange the leaves staggered or emanating in a straight line as you desire. Using a round brush, make small red or dark-pink rosebuds or bouquets in the center of the "+." Use all the colors in your palette for the flowers and double- or triple-load your paintbrush to add dimension and shades. Add the leaves at all four points of the "+." Divide the top and sides of the dresser in half lengthwise to paint their trellis patterns. Make a large flower arrangement in the center of the dresser top. When your hand painting dries, apply two or more coats of sealer to the entire piece (Step 2). When that dries, replace the old hardware, and insert the drawers. Embellish the edges with gold wax. Remove the tape, and finish with sealer.

2 Once the paint dries, apply two or more coats of a clear sealer, such as a water-based polyurethane, which will not yellow. Once the sealer is thoroughly dry, replace the hardware and insert the drawers.

TIPS ON PAINTING STRIPES

Stripes are among the most attractive painted effects you can add to a surface. Broad, even stripes, such as the ones used on this dresser, can go on fairly quickly and evenly. If your hand isn't particularly steady, roll on the paint rather than use a brush to apply it. You can find narrow rollers in paint and craft shops, or you can cut down a standard-size roller to the desired width of the stripe. It's best to use a thick paint instead of a thin glaze because you have to make one uninterrupted pass with the roller. Avoid running the roller up and down. Load the roller from a paint tray. Start at the top, and run the roller straight down (or across) the surface. For a neat look, mask the edges before applying the paint.

masking tapes

Designing for Special Needs

Parents of children with physical challenges know that an inaccessible environment is frustrating. But sometimes a few thoughtful adaptations can make a child's room comfortable and easier to live in without sacrificing any of the fun stuff that makes it a special place that is all his own. By eliminating the obstacles that make him constantly dependent upon others, you can help your special-needs kid develop a can-do attitude that will carry him successfully through life.

When you think about it, gearing a room for use by any child is essentially an exercise in creating an adapted environment. Most of the time, it only takes common sense. Ordinarily, we lower storage, adjust mirrors to an appropriate height, keep electrical cords and other objects out of the aisles. We look for furniture that's easy to use, beds and chairs that are accessible to a child, handles, knobs, or pulls that a child's hands can grab. All of these efforts are intended to make children independent, comfortable, and safe. All children are remarkably resourceful when it comes to fulfilling their own agenda. But all children also need a little help to get them there. A special-needs child may need just a bit more.

Introduce color contrasts and lots of non-glaring natural light into the room of a visually impaired child. In this room, note how the white furniture contrasts well with the vivid color of the wall. Because the room is on the first floor, the homeowner replaced one large window with a bank of smaller units so that the sunlight could enter the space without sacrificing privacy.

Levels of Ability

The first thing to do is determine what areas of independence require your special consideration. Analyze your child in terms of the following:

* *Fine motor skills.* They affect the ability to flip light switches, turn doorknobs, contain work on a smaller work surface, operate stereo and television controls, and manipulate a computer keyboard.

* *Upper body strength.* This is needed to open doors, pull drawers, and carry heavier toys.

* *Extent of reach.* This will determine the ability to retrieve objects, control lighting, and other electronics.

* *Stamina.* This affects the ability to handle a wheelchair, climb stairs, open a heavy door, lift one's self in and out of bed, and cross the room in some cases.

* *Gross motor-skill level.* This will determine the ability to maneuver a wheelchair or walker precisely and negotiate the room.

In addition to physical limitations, a sensory deprivation such as visual impairment, blindness, hearing loss, and deafness will require some room adaptations. Allergic or asthmatic children also can benefit from rooms that are tailored to their specific needs for a dust- and allergen-free environment.

Your child's needs and the adaptations they require may be highly specific to her. But there are steps you can take that can improve the livability of your child's room in general. Some adaptations are merely logical and can be put in place with ordinary materials; others may require specific products. Consult the Resources, page 165, which may be helpful if you need to locate a special device. And don't forget to ask for your child's cooperation when you're planning the room's design. You can't put yourself in her place, so ask her to point out things that may be helpful or to demonstrate how much turn-around room is necessary for her wheelchair. Ask what you can do to make moving around and using the furniture easier.

Doors can pose a problem for some kids. Openings should be wide enough to accommodate a wheelchair or walker, and handles and knobs should be easy to operate.

THE BEDROOM DOOR

The bedroom door is primarily to provide access when it's open and privacy when it's closed. But the inability to clear the door with a wheelchair or a walker or to turn the door handle presents a large problem. It compromises your child's freedom to move in and out of his own room at will and without help.

To make a door opening wheelchair- and walker-accessible, so that both equipment and little hands can pass through unscathed, the opening must be at least 32 inches wide. If widening the doorway is not possible, you can gain a few inches by reinstalling the door on offset or swing-clear hinges. There should also be a clearance of 18 inches of wall space next to the door handle. A tight space will make it difficult if not impossible to grab and turn the handle or knob. If clearance is a problem, you could exchange the door for one that can be installed in the opposite direction. (Replace a door with a right-hand swing for one with a left-hand swing.) Replacing a standard door with a pocket door (one that slides into the wall) is another idea. An automatic door that works by remote control or on sensors can solve the problem, too, but the cost of one is much greater than that of a standard door.

Door hardware can be another stumbling block. If gripping and turning knobs is a problem, replace them with lever or loop-type hardware. Add-on lever extensions can convert an ordinary knob. You can get one that installs permanently or one that travels with the child to give access to doors throughout the house. Give any solution you use the closed-fist test — that is, make sure you can open it easily with just one hand, closed into a fist. If your child has the use of only one arm, it may be helpful to reinstall the door so that the handle is easily accessible. You

can apply many of these ideas to the closet door as well. The weight of the door can be a problem if your child has limited strength or stamina. Look for a lighter-weight hollow-core door to replace an existing solid-wood door.

Also, getting the door open is not much use if the threshold immediately presents another barrier. The best plan is to eliminate it completely.

LAYOUT AND FURNISHINGS

A wheelchair needs a 5-foot radius of space to turn around. Children using walkers need plenty of space to manipulate their equipment, too. So when you're organizing the layout of the room for a child who uses one of these items, make good use of the available wall space. The basic plan should be to keep the center area of the room clear, and to arrange all the furniture and activity stations against the walls. If the room is shared and contains two beds, make sure a 36-inch aisle exists between the beds and to any exit or activity area.

Clear the aisles and the center of the room. Make sure your child can maneuver his wheelchair or walker in the space.

Smart Tip

FLOORING. For ease of exit and entry, make sure that any transition from a hard floor surface to carpeting is made gradually, using metal threshold strips. Any carpeting and matting should measure no more than a half inch thick. And because wheelchairs and walkers can take a toll on the baseboards and make unsightly marks on the wall, consider running the carpeting 4 or 5 inches up the wall.

Because it may not be possible for some special-needs children to play on the floor, install large desktop surfaces for games and hobbies. These surfaces can also serve homework projects and personal grooming tasks. Keep appropriate materials close by their designated station for easy access. In the case of older children, equip the tabletop with electrical outlets he can reach (a computer surge-protector strip, for example) and be sure switches to control task lighting sources are also within reach. A tabletop for a wheelchair-bound adult should measure between 28 to 34 inches high; you'll have to measure to find the height that is comfortable for your child. The depth of the table should be designed to be convenient to its user's ability to reach. Knee space should be 27 inches high, 30 inches wide, and 19 inches deep. A single large desktop, cantilevered from the wall and divided into different activity stations, is another good idea. It makes traveling between stations easy. Storage crates and shelves that house the materials to be used at each station can be used to visually section off the different zones.

If a child who uses a walker must stand, or is more comfortable standing, to perform certain activities, look for adjustable-height tables that will accommodate her needs as she grows. An artist's drawing board might work for this application. Furniture designed to function as a freestanding kitchen or work cart is another option.

Bending down to pick up toys or materials that fall or roll off work surfaces is frequently impossible for a child with special needs. Attach hook-and-loop-type strips at the top and sides of the work surface and to each item that will be used in that station to eliminate this problem. This is also a good solution if the child uses items on a wheelchair tray. If the item is too large or you don't want to attach something as permanent as the hook-and-loop strips (on a computer keyboard, for example), try large C-clamps from a hardware store. If the room is too small to accommodate a series of workstations, use a variety of wheelchair trays, customized for each activity.

Assuming Controls. Controls for lighting the room must be both reachable and workable. There are devices available at children's product stores that can replace an existing light-switch plate for one that is mounted lower on the wall. If you have light switches lowered, raise the level of the electrical

A lowered countertop with knee room underneath is a great surface for coloring or reading a book with siblings or friends.

outlets at the same time. Adapters that make electrical outlets easy to find for the visually impaired and easy to use where fine motor skills are problematic are also available. One such product extends the outlet so that it protrudes an inch from the wall. The raised surface protects hands from potential shocks and creates a channel that guides the plug into the outlet. Lamps also can be adapted for kids with limited grasping ability by attaching spoked-style switches to existing ones. Look on the Internet or in related catalogs for many of these items.

If your child lacks the fine motor ability to manipulate any switch, consider a motion-sensor light as an ambient light source — it can be installed on a timer so that it shuts off at bedtime. The good old device that allows you to clap-on and clap-off lights is another possibility. It can be used to turn on a stereo, television, or computer as well. There are many products that allow you to tailor electronic devices in a room for a person with specific limitations. The Education Development Center of the National Center to Improve Practice has compiled an extensive list of adaptive technology for computers to aid students who are visually impaired. (See the Resources section on pages 165–168.)

ACCESSIBLE STORAGE

Just as you would lower storage to accommodate little children, you can raise it to suit a child who cannot get down to floor level. Stacking crates are perfect for this purpose. Lower crates can hold seldom-used items or the things you use to care for your child, while the upper crates contain toys, games, books, and the usual array of kid stuff. For visually impaired children, color code the crates to help them find just what they're looking for — for example, keep action figures in a red crate, books in a yellow crate, and so on.

LIGHTING AND COLORS FOR THE VISUALLY IMPAIRED. Visually impaired kids benefit from bright light, but are hindered more than other kids by glare. Keep reflective surfaces, those with glossy finishes, to a minimum. Position mirrors, the computer, and TV so that they will not pick up glare from window light or artificial lighting sources.

Bright contrasts — not necessarily bright colors — are most readily appreciated by kids with low vision. Use pretty contrasts for decoration. Reserve bright "warning" colors, such as orange, to mark changes in floor grade or "do not touch" spots.

Find creative ways to color-code items in the room of a visually impaired child. This artfully painted desk can be adapted to any child's needs.

Look for dressers with drawers that open and close with a minimum of effort. Ones on rollers are perfect. Drawers constructed of lightweight material such as plastic, while usually too flimsy to stand up to "kid-force," work well for a child with limited strength. If drawers are too difficult to handle, store clothing in cubbies attached to the wall at an accessible height. Wall-mounted cabinets usually found in the kitchen make great close-away storage for kids who can't maneuver drawers but can manage the cabinet doors.

Closet bars can be lowered. Where the bar is permanently attached, simply install another below it. Automated devices

that rotate clothing and make finding an item easier, are also available. As long as it is kept neatly, clothing can be hung on a rack located outside the closet. This is much more accessible for kids with wheelchairs and walkers. Shoes and accessories hang up neatly on shaker pegs attached to the wall at the child's level.

Allergy and Asthma Issues

The answer to keeping a bedroom free of allergens — agents that cause allergic reactions to dust mites, food particles, animal dander, bits of plants and insects, mold and fungus, and bits of fabrics — is to create an environment inhospitable to the dust that carries them. The following Smart Steps will prepare the room initially; conscientious cleaning will keep it that way.

SMART STEPS — **ONE: Seal the bed.** Start by covering the bed's mattress and box spring in the airtight, washable plastic zipper covers made for this purpose. Pillows made of foam are preferable, but not the most comfortable. If your child needs a more comfortable headrest, experiment with nonallergenic synthetic pillows. Avoid feather and down pillows completely. Like the mattress, cover the pillow with an airtight plastic case. Natural wool and cotton-fiber blankets are best. Wash all bedding weekly in very hot water to kill mites and remove skin particles. Some experts recommend changing to a clean pillowcase daily.

TWO: Go easy with fabrics. Fabric accessories with their pleats, folds, and nap are notorious dust collectors. To combat this, keep window treatments spare and ban upholstered furnishings from the room. A simple roller blind, which is easier to dust than the slats of mini-blinds, will suffice. Find one that is printed to coordinate with the room. If you use a vinyl shade, you can stencil a design onto it. Fabric paint will work for your project if you use a blind made of canvas or another no-nap material.

THREE: Choose a hard floor surface. Carpeting collects dust and the chemicals in its foam-rubber padding can cause an allergic reaction, too. A hardwood floor is best. When it comes time to have the floor refinished, visit Grandma or go away for the weekend, leaving the windows open for several days, if possible. Make sure the varnish has a low VOC (volatile organic compounds) rating. Get the floor professionally cleaned or rent a vacuum with a HEPA (high-efficiency particulate arrestance) filtration system to remove all the sanding particles. Depending on the type of adhesive used, a vinyl floor is also suitable for this kind of installation—and it can just be given a daily mopping. Frequently washed, low-pile area rugs will soften the floor for play.

To create this allergen-free haven, opposite, low-VOC (volatile organic compounds) paint was used. A ceiling fan keeps air circulating. Peeled-log bunk beds, right, keep it fun.

FOUR: Clear the air. Dry air is best for kids with allergies. Don't wait until the dog days of summer to use an air-conditioner; start running it as soon as allergy season draws near in the early spring. To maintain an ideal humidity level of less than 50 percent, you may need a dehumidifier. Clean filters frequently and replace them when needed. If allergies are severe, a HEPA filtration unit may help.

FIVE: Eliminate upholstery. Every time a plush seat is used, millions of tiny particles are propelled into the air your child breathes. Solid-wood or metal furnishings are easy to keep dust-free. Avoid heavy lacquers, paint or varnish, particleboard, or wood veneers that can emit fumes into the air.

Open displays of collectibles are okay in an allergy sufferer's room but will require regular, thorough dusting. Bare floors are best as well.

SIX: Banish animals. Both the living kind and the plush variety are bad news for allergy sufferers. Even if the family pet is tolerable for the allergic child, keep him out of the bedroom. For a young child, choose one or two stuffed animals that are machine-washable to keep around. If a non-machine-washable favorite already exists, pop it into the freezer ever so often to kill mites. Otherwise, wash the stuffed toys regularly with the bedding.

In general, the allergy sufferer's room should be spare and easy to clean. Keep knickknacks to a minimum and behind glass doors when your child is old enough to coexist safely with glass. The fewer surfaces the room contains, the fewer places to breed for dust mites and mold. The easier it is to clean, the cleaner it will be kept. If possible, establish play, homework, or other activity space elsewhere in the house, and limit bedroom furnishings to a bed and dresser. A child spends many hours in the room where she sleeps, so it's important to make it clean, comfortable, and allergen-free.

Fine Tuning

Regardless of the nature of a child's physical challenges, strict upkeep of the room is vital to its functionality. Parents of allergic children must be fanatical about keeping the room dust-free. The best wheelchair-access design in the world will be foiled if clutter bars the way. Clutter can be downright dangerous to blind or visually impaired kids. It is imperative that the belongings of a blind or visually impaired child are returned to their usual places in the room. Inasmuch as is possible and age-appropriate, disabled children should share in the responsibility for their room's upkeep. Helping to care for their own room is an ideal training ground to learn practices that will make them independent later in life.

DON'T FORGET THE DETAILS

Whether it is breathing through a nebulizer for 15 minutes several times a day, receiving therapeutic massage, performing exercises, or enduring slow-drip intravenous medications, chances are they come to resent this time away from the important business of being a kid. While it may not be possible to eliminate these routines, you can make the time spent pass

Make storage accessible. For kids with little upper-body strength, a lightweight door on a cabinet or armoire may be easier to open than a heavy drawer.

more quickly. Customize the room so that it can provide some kind of entertainment during these treatments. A TV and VCR are perfect for this purpose. Consider wall-mounting the TV if that makes it easier to view. Where sight is impaired or viewing is not possible, look for books on tape. You might also consider setting up an aquarium. If a treatment is rendered while your child lies prone in bed, a well-placed TV and game controls might be doable to provide a distraction.

For a child who is unable to help herself out of bed in the morning (also appropriate for one who receives treatment lying down in bed) consider investing in an overhead projector. You can load it each at night with a "surprise" transparency. Teaching-aids stores and catalogs have some ready-made transparencies available. You can create your own with transparency sheets and erasable markers or by transferring materials onto transparency sheets with a copier machine. Adjust the projector so that the image appears on the ceiling. Affix the controls to the bed so that she can turn it on herself, or you can turn it on once she's awake. If she can control it and withstand the position change, investing in an adjustable bed and affixing a TV to the wall may be another option.

CHAPTER 10

Bathrooms for Baby on Up

Bathing is a key part in everyone's life, and children are no exception. The bathroom, therefore, is an important environment. One that is designed around a child's smaller size enables him to move most effortlessly into taking charge of his own personal hygiene. Special safety concerns should always take precedence over other design elements. If you share a bathroom with your child, take prudent steps to accommodate his size and needs.

Most newer homes contain a second bath, which is often designated for the children in the family. What should be included in it depends on the ages and number of children who will use it. If your child is lucky enough to have the room all to herself, plan it for her growing and changing needs. Anticipate the storage and lighting requirements of a teenage girl's grooming habits, for example. If more than one child will share the bath, consider their genders, and whether they will use the room at the same time. How many lavatories do they need? At least two. The best designs for shared bathrooms include compartmentalized spaces—one for the toilet, one for the bath, perhaps one for a separate shower, one for the lavatories, plus storage. If this isn't feasible, at least try to set the toilet apart. It will make the day's beginning and ending less hectic.

Designed for flexible use, the life span of this bath's decorating is extended by fixtures in a neutral tone. Bright color accents appear in the bath toys and playthings. The tub-and-shower area is decorated with a colorful tile mural and border; its fish-aquarium design is charming but not childish. Contemporary white faucet sets are easy-to-operate at any age.

Soft furnishings set the tone. A gathered sink skirt pads the sink's hard edges. A hand-painted frame dresses up a basic mirror.

There are fixtures on the market that are tailored for child use, but you may not want to make the investment in something that will have to be replaced once your child matures or leaves home. As always, it's a matter of choice. If you want to make the room appealing to the younger set but your funds are limited, look into wallpaper patterns that have a juvenile theme and use lively, kid-friendly colors and accessories.

BATHROOM BASICS

There are lots of things you can do to make any bathroom practical, comfortable, and safe for family members of all ages. When you're planning to build or renovate a bath that will be used by a child, careful consideration should be given to both of you, but pay particular attention to the age-specific needs of the youngster.

INFANTS AND TODDLERS
The baby's bathroom should be a warm, draft-free environment, but you should organize the space around your needs for bathing the baby, as well. You'll want everything right at hand

so you can keep a constant vigil. Remember: A child can drown in less than 2 inches of water in a baby tub or toilet, or even in a bucket filled with water.

Appropriate furnishings include a comfortable seating area where you can dry the baby or towel a toddler, a convenient place to house the baby bath, and ample storage for shampoo, wash cloths, towels, diapers, toys, a hamper, and a diaper pail.

Consider your own comfort when positioning the baby bath. Counter height probably will be most comfortable, or you may consider a freestanding bathing unit. Install an anti-scald faucet, which contains a device that keeps water temperate. Because a child's skin is thinner and more tender than an adult's, it can be burned within 3 seconds after coming into contact with water that's over 120 degrees Fahrenheit. Fixtures equipped with a pressure-balancing feature will maintain the same degree of hotness even when cold-water flow is reduced (when you flush the toilet, for example). Style-wise, a single-lever faucet, as opposed to two separate valves, is much easier for a child to use when regulating water flow and temperature. You can preset some of them, as well.

A hand-held shower device that allows you to position the showerhead at a convenient level can be retrofitted onto a conventional showerhead or installed separately. Look for one that's been designed for children to handle.

Once you start to bathe the baby in the tub, you'll want to make it slip-resistant. A textured surface helps. You can easily add this with anti-slip decals and mats. Install soft covers over the faucet and spout so that a little one can't be bruised. Parents can protect themselves by using a mat that extends over the side of the tub to cushion arms that are holding up and bathing the baby. Part of the mat also rests on the floor to pad adult knees.

It's a good idea to install easy-care wallcovering and flooring. From the first moment a toddler learns to splash, all claims to toughness are tested. Classic selections include tiles, waterproof vinyl wallcovering that has a built-in mildewcide, solid-surfacing material or a fiberglass tub surround, and gloss or semi-gloss paint, also with a mildewcide.

Lower, one-piece toilets that hug closer to the wall and have an elongated bowl make toilet training a little easier. They are scaled better for a child while being comfortable for adults.

PRESCHOOLERS

Toilet training and the beginning of self-grooming mark this stage, necessitating a few changes in the way your child will use the bathroom. Tubs and toys seem to go together here. You'll need more room for toy storage; gear it to something your child can access himself, such as a plastic basket that can be kept inside a vanity cabinet or on the floor of the linen closet. You'll also need a place to keep a small step stool when it's not in use as a booster in front of the lav. If you're renovating or building a new bathroom for a child, consider installing a lav into a vanity or countertop that is built at a lower height.

Because the standard rule of thumb is to install a mirror 8 inches above a standard-height vanity countertop (to avoid splatters), you may want to include a standing mirror or one

Plan now for later. This tub is equipped with an adjustable, hand-held spray — good for bathing toddlers and an easy reach for older, more self-reliant children. A conventional fixed shower head is available as well.

that extends from the wall at a proper height to suit your child. To encourage neatness, a towel rack that is within a child's reach is another good idea. A low freestanding rack works well, too.

SCHOOL-AGE KIDS

Socializing skills in school reinforce the needs for individual identity at home, including specific grooming styles as a child gets older. Storage niches once devoted to bathtub toys can be used for hair ribbons, special soaps and shampoos, or other toiletries. Keep electrical appliances, such as hair dryers and steam rollers, or electric shavers out of the room until your child is old enough to handle them responsibly and understand the hazards posed by electricity and water.

More About Shared Spaces. The crunch starts when kids begin toilet training and continues through the school years when everybody has to get bathed, dressed, and out of the house at the same time. To cope with the increased demands, create private areas within the room, such as the separate bathing, grooming, and toilet areas suggested earlier. Color-code towels and accessories so that everyone can clearly see

what belongs to each person who uses the room. Finally, move certain activities to other rooms. Dressing and grooming can be done in the bedroom, for example.

Whether your home has one small bathroom that is shared by all or a separate bathroom for each member of the family, there are steps you can take to make the room efficient.

SMART STEPS

ONE: **Plan storage.** If you can't afford the space of a linen closet within the room, add shelving to hold extra towels, bars of soap, and other necessities. Small storage niches created between the wall studs make handy spots for shampoo and toiletries. Mount hooks or pegged racks to the wall or behind the door for hanging extra towels or robes. New medicine cabinets come with extra deep shelves that are large enough to hold rolls of toilet paper or bulky blow-dryers.

TWO: **Consider a better way to use space.** Cramped floor space? Replace the bathroom door with a pocket door to free up floor space that might allow you to create a separate shower stall or a double vanity.

THREE: **Remember to light and ventilate the room properly.** Besides general lighting, you and your child will need good task lighting for grooming. Proper ventilation is important, too. Invest in a good exhaust fan; not only will it make the room's air quality healthier and surfaces less slick but it will help to maintain materials that can be ruined by water buildup and mildew.

FOUR: **Make the room safe.** Refer to the Smart Tip box on the opposite page for guidelines regarding bathroom safety.

Handy drawers and cubbyholes, top and right, are the answer to children's bathroom storage. Above, a low shelf in the shower puts bathing and shampoo supplies within a child's reach.

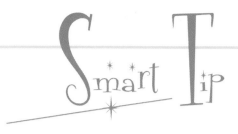

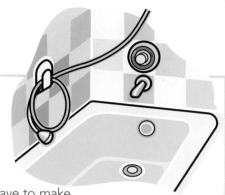

BATHROOM SAFETY. Here's a list of things that you should have to make sure any bathroom that is intended for a child's use is safe and comfortable.

TUB & SHOWER AREAS

▶ Safety glazing on glass doors

▶ Doors that are hinged to swing out into the room

▶ Grab bars at adult and child heights

▶ A shower seat

TOILETS & WATER CLOSETS

▶ No lock on the water-closet door

▶ Locked toilet lid

▶ Tip-resistant training step stool

▶ Toilet-paper holder installed within the child's reach

PLUMBING

▶ Water valves within easy reach

▶ Single-lever controls

▶ Anti-scald and pressure-balanced faucets

▶ Adjustable child-size hand shower

ELECTRIC

▶ Ground-fault circuit interrupters (GFCIs) on all outlets

▶ Covered receptacles

▶ Vapor-proof light fixtures installed out of the child's reach

▶ Low-voltage task lighting

▶ Night light

CABINET & COUNTER SURFACES

▶ Small doors that can be easily opened

▶ Child-proof locks

▶ Locked medicine cabinet

▶ No more than 8-inch-deep cabinets installed over the toilet

▶ Rounded corners and edges

▶ Seating for drying off and dressing

FLOORING

▶ Non-slip surface

▶ Water-resistant surface

▶ Anchors for area rugs and mats

WINDOWS & DOORS

▶ Doors that swing into the room

▶ Door locks that can be opened from the outside

▶ Safety bars on all windows

APPENDIX: KIDS' ROOMS TEMPLATES

Window and Door Templates

Windows

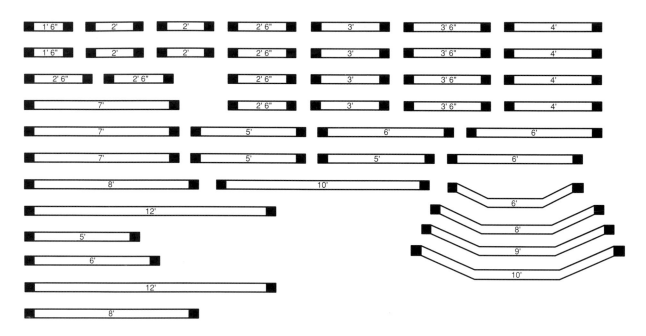

Doors

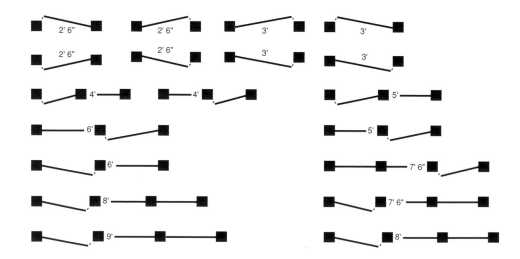

Appendix: Furniture Templates

Beds

Crib 30"x54"	twin bed with headboard 44"x75" mattress 39"x75"	double bed with headboard 59"x75" mattress 54"x75"	queen size with headboard 64"x80" mattress 60"x80"	king size with headboard 83"x80" mattress 78"x80"

Case Goods

Chest 30x21x44 to 56 · Chest 36x21x36 · Chest 42x21x44 to 56 · Chest 48x21x36 · Chest 66x21x36

Chest 30"x17"x36" · Chest 36"x17"x36" · Chest 42"x17"x36" · Armoire 38"x21" · Armoire 42"x24"

Chest 48"x17"x36" · Chest 60"x17"x36" · Chest 66"x17"x36"

Chest 36"x13" · Chest 52"x13" · Bookcase 30"x12" · Bookcase 36"x12" · Bookcase 48"x12" · Bookcase 60"x12"

Storage 19"x19" · Storage 26"x19" · Storage 36"x19" · Storage 52"x19" · Storage & Changing Table 36"x21"x36" · dressing table 46"x20" · dressing table 42"x22"

Appendix: Furniture Templates

Built-In Cabinets

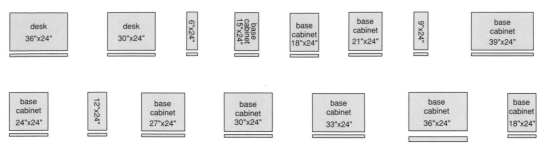

Tables and Desks

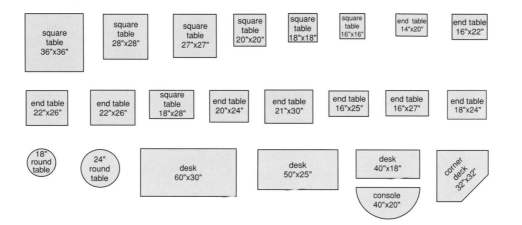

Chairs and Ottomans

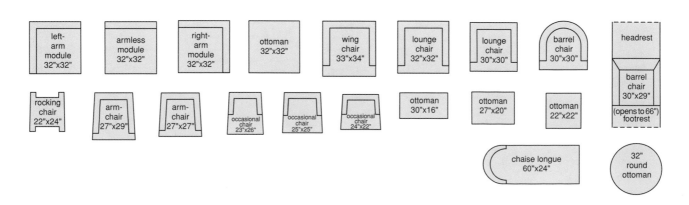

Appendix: Furniture Templates

Sofas, Love Seats, and Sofa Beds

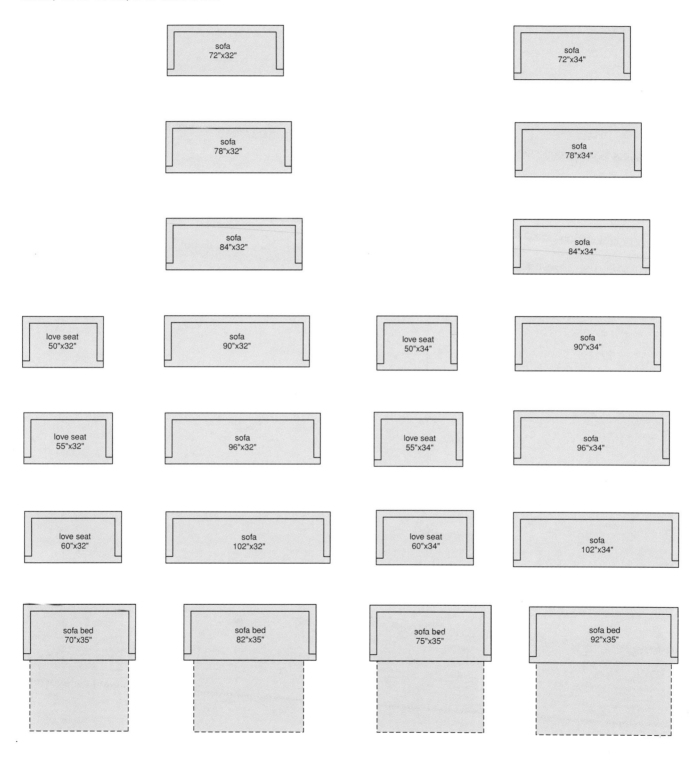

Scale: 1 square=1 foot

GLOSSARY

Acetate: The plastic sheet material often used for making stencils.

Accent Lighting: A type of lighting that highlights an area or object to emphasize that aspect of a room's character.

Accessible Designs: Those that accommodate persons with physical disabilities.

Acrylic Paint: A water-soluble paint with a plastic polymer (acrylic) binder.

Adaptable Designs: Those that can be easily changed or adjusted to accommodate a person with disabilities.

Alkyd Paint: A paint-thinner-soluble paint that contains a binder made of soya or urethane resins (alkyds). It is often imprecisely called "oil-based" paint. Alkyds have replaced linseed oil, which was used as a binder in oil-based paint.

Analogous Scheme: *See Harmonious Color Scheme.*

Ambient Lighting: General or background illumination that surrounds a room, such as the light produced by a ceiling fixture or cove lighting.

Armoire: A large, often ornate, cupboard or wardrobe that is used for storage.

Backlighting: Illumination coming from a source behind or adjacent to an object.

Blender Brushes: Specialty brushes used to blend and soften all types of wet painted surfaces.

Box Pleat: A double pleat, underneath which the edges fold toward each other.

Broadloom: A wide loom for weaving carpeting that is 54 inches wide or more.

Built-in: Any element, such as a bookcase or cabinetry, that is built into a wall or an existing frame.

Case Goods: Furniture used for storage, including cabinets, dressers, and desks.

Chaise Longue: A chair with back support and a seat long enough for outstretched legs.

Cheesecloth: A loosely woven, coarse cotton gauze used to create different textures as well as to blend and smooth wet paint over a surface.

Clear Top Coat: A transparent finishing layer of protection applied over a decorated surface.

Clearance: The amount of space between two fixtures, the centerlines of two fixtures, or a fixture and an obstacle, such as a wall. Clearances may be mandated by codes.

Code: A locally or nationally enforced mandate regarding structural design, materials, plumbing, or electrical systems that state what you can or cannot do when you build or remodel. Codes are intended to protect standards of health, safety, and land use.

Color Scheme: A group of colors used together to create visual harmony in a space.

Color Washing: The technique of applying layers of heavily thinned glaze to a surface to produce a faded, transparent wash of color.

Color Wheel: A pie-shaped diagram showing the range and relationships of pigment and dye colors. Three equidistant wedge-shaped slices are the primaries; in between are the secondary and tertiary colors into which the primaries combine. Though represented as discrete slices, the hues form a continuum.

Combing: A technique that involves dragging a plastic or metal comb through wet paint or glaze in order to simulate texture or to create a pattern.

Complementary Colors: Hues directly opposite each other on the color wheel. As the strongest contrasts, complements tend to intensify each other. A color can be grayed by mixing it with its complement.

Contemporary: Any modern design (after 1920) that does not contain or refer to traditional elements of the past.

Contrast: The art of assembling colors with different values and intensities and in different proportions to create a dynamic scheme.

Cornice: A projecting, decorative box installed above a window, designed to cover a curtain rod.

Daybed: A bed made up to appear as a sofa. It usually has a frame that consists of a headboard, a footboard, and a sideboard along the back.

Decoupage: The technique of applying cut-out paper or fabric motifs to a surface, and then coating the images with varnish or decoupage medium.

Decoupage Medium: A smooth and glossy glue-like liquid used to apply cut-out paper or fabric images to a surface or an object. It is used as both an adhesive and a top coat.

Dimmer Switch: A switch that can vary the intensity of the light it controls.

Distressed Finish: A decorative paint technique in which the final paint coat is sanded and battered to produce an aged appearance.

Dovetail: A joinery method in which wedge-shaped parts are interlocked to form a tight bond. This joint is commonly used on furniture parts, such as drawers.

Dowel: A short cylinder, made of wood, metal, or plastic, that fits into corresponding holes bored in two pieces of wood, creating a joint.

Dragging: A technique that involves pulling a special long-bristled brush through wet paint or glaze to create fine lines or narrow stripes.

Etagère: Freestanding or hanging shelves for displaying small objects.

Faux: The French word for "false." With regard to painted finishes, it is used to describe any technique in which paint is manipulated on a surface to imitate the appearance of another substance, such as wood or stone.

Flat Finish: The absence of sheen after a paint or finish dries.

Fluorescent Lighting: A glass tube coated on the interior with phosphor, a chemical compound that emits light when activated by ultraviolet energy. Air in the tube is replaced with a combination of argon gas and a small amount of mercury. Lamps are also circular and bulb shaped.

Focal Point: The dominant element in a room or design, usually the first to catch your eye.

Frieze: A horizontal band at the top of the wall or just below the cornice.

Glaze: A thinned-down, translucent emulsion that may or may not contain pigment (color).

Glossy Finish: The appearance of sheen after a paint or finish dries.

Graining Comb: A flexible steel or plastic device with random-sized tines or teeth. It is dragged through wet glaze or paint to create striated or grained surfaces. A common hair comb makes a workable substitute.

Ground-Fault Circuit Interrupter (GFCI): A safety circuit breaker that compares the amount of current entering a receptacle with the amount leaving. If there is a discrepancy of 0.005 volt, the GFCI breaks the circuit in a fraction of a second.

GFCIs are required by the National Electrical Code in kitchens, bathrooms, laundries—and in any other rooms with plumbing.

Hardware: Wood, plastic, or metal-plated trim found on the exterior of furniture, such as knobs, handles, and decorative trim.

Harmonious Color Scheme: Also called analogous, a combination focused on neighboring hues on the color wheel. The shared underlying color generally gives such schemes a coherent flow.

Hue: Another term for specific points on the pure, clear range of the color wheel.

Incandescent Lighting: A bulb (lamp) that converts electric power into light by passing electric current through a filament of tungsten wire.

Indirect Lighting: A more subdued type of lighting that is not head-on, but rather reflected against another surface such as a ceiling.

Lambrequin: Drapery that hangs from a shelf, such as a mantel, or covering the top of a window or a door. This term is sometimes used interchangeably with valance.

Laminate: One or more thin layers of durable plastic that is bonded to a fabric or a material—Formica, for example.

Latex Paint: Paint that contains either acrylic or vinyl resins or a combination of the two. High-quality latex paints contain 100-percent acrylic resin. Latex paint is water-soluble and dries quickly.

Lining Brush: A thin, flexible, long-bristled brush used for fine lining and detail work.

Love Seat: A sofa-like piece of furniture that consists of seating for two.

Modular: Units of a standard size, such as pieces of a sofa, that can be fitted together in a number of ways.

Molding: An architectural band that can either trim a line where materials join or create a linear decoration. It is typically made of wood, but metal, plaster, or polymer (plastic) is also used.

Mortise-and-Tenon Joinery: A hole (mortise) cut into a piece of wood that receives a projecting piece (tenon) to create a joint. It is often used in fine furnituremaking.

Orientation: The placement of any object or space, such as a window, a door, or a room, and its relationship to the points on a compass.

Overglaze: A thin glaze added as a final step to a decorative paint finish. It can be a thinner version of the base coat or it can be mixed in a different color.

Panel: A flat, rectangular piece of material that forms part of a wall, door, or cabinet. Typically made of wood, it is usually framed by a border and either raised or recessed.

Parquet: Inlaid woodwork arranged to form a geometric pattern on a floor. It consists of small blocks of hardwood, which are often stained in contrasting colors.

Pattern Matching: To align a repeating pattern when joining together two pieces of fabric or wallpaper.

Polyurethane: A tough, hard-wearing coating made of synthetic resins. It serves as a good top coat or finish and can be applied over most types of paint, except artist's oils.

Primary Color: Red, blue, or yellow, which can't be produced in pigments by mixing other colors. Primaries plus black and white, in turn, combine to make all the other hues.

Primers: Primers prepare surfaces for painting by making them more uniform in texture and giving them "tooth."

Sea Sponge: A natural sponge, not to be confused with the cellulose variety used in households. It is used to apply paint in a technique called sponging.

Sealers: These products are applied to porous surfaces before painting in order to form a durable, nonabsorbent barrier between the surface and the paint. This avoids a rough, uneven, dull finish.

Secondary Color: A mix of two primaries. The secondary colors are orange, green, and purple.

Semigloss Finish: These paints have a hard, slightly glossy finish that is light reflective, somewhere between gloss and eggshell.

Shade: A color to which black or gray has been added to make it darker.

Sheen: The quality of paint that reflects light when it is dry.

Slipcover: A fabric or plastic cover that can be draped or tailored to fit over a piece of furniture.

Spattering: Applying random dots of paint over a surface by striking a saturated brush or by rubbing paint through a screen.

Sponging: A paint technique that involves using a sponge to apply or take off paint.

Stencil: A cut-out pattern.

Stenciling: Creating an image or a motif, often in a repeated pattern, by painting a cut-out pattern.

Task Lighting: Lighting that concentrates in specific areas for tasks, such as preparing food, applying makeup, reading, or doing crafts.

Thinner: A liquid that is mixed with paint to make it less thick. Mineral spirits may be used for alkyd paints and water for latex paint.

Tint: A color to which white or light gray has been added to make it lighter.

Tone: Degree of lightness or darkness of a color. A color to which gray has been added to change its value.

Tongue-and-Groove Joinery: A wood joinery technique in which a protruding end (tongue) or edge fits into a recess (groove), locking the two pieces together.

Track Lighting: Lighting that utilizes a fixed band that supplies a current to movable light fixtures.

Trompe L'oeil: Literally meaning "fool the eye"; a painted mural in which realistic images and the illusion of more space are created. Also, a painted surface that convincingly mimics reality.

Turning: Wood that is cut on a lathe into a round object with a distinctive profile. Furniture legs, posts, rungs, etc., are usually made in this way.

Uplight: Also used to describe the lights themselves, this is actually the term for light that is directed upward toward the ceiling or the upper part of walls.

Valance: A short length of drapery that hangs along the top part of a window, with or without a curtain underneath.

Value: In relation to a scale of grays ranging from black to white, this is the term to describe the lightness (tints) or darkness (shades) of a color.

Veneer: High-quality wood that is cut into very thin sheets for use as a surface material.

Wash: A thinned-out latex or acrylic paint.

Welt: A cord, often covered by fabric, that is used as an elegant trim on cushions, slipcovers, etc.

RESOURCES

ASSOCIATIONS

Better Sleep Council (BSC)
333 Commerce St.
Alexandria, VA 22314
Phone: 703/683-8371
Fax: 703/683-8371
Web site: www.bettersleep.org
The Better Sleep Council (BSC) is a nonprofit organization that is devoted to educating the public about the importance of sleep to good health and quality of life. Visit their Web site for more information, or contact them for a free 16-page color brochure on the importance of good sleep to your quality of life and some tips on how to get a good night's sleep.

Consumer Product Safety Commission (CPSC)
US Consumer Product Safety Commission
Washington, DC 20207-0001
Phone: 800/638-2772
Web site: cpsc.gov
CPSC, an independent federal regulatory agency, helps keep American families safe by reducing the risk of injury or death from consumer products. Call or visit their Web site to request product safety information or to report unsafe products. There is even a special section on their Web site devoted to kids.

Juvenile Products Manufacturers Association
236 Route 38 West
Suite 100
Moorestown, NJ 08057
Web site: www.jpma.org
This national trade organization represents companies in the United States, Canada, and Mexico that manufacture and/or import infant products such as cribs, bedding, and a wide range of accessories and decorative items. Write or visit their Web site for "Safe & Sound for Baby," a 20-page brochure that outlines safe product usage and safety measures to ensure baby's safety.

National Center to Improve Practice (NCIP)
Education Development Center, Inc.
Newton, MA
Web site: www.edc.org/NCIP
Visit this Web site to learn how to enhance educational programming for our youngest students with disabilities. Early childhood educators are discovering the power of technology for promoting growth in communication, social interaction, and cognitive development among preschoolers.

National Safety Council (NSC)
1121 Spring Lake Dr.
Itasca, IL 60143-3201
Phone: 800/621-7619
Web site: www.nsc.org
The National Safety Council is a nonprofit public service organization dedicated to improving the safety, health, and environmental well-being of all people. Their Web site includes different programs that focus on safety in and surrounding the home.

USEFUL WEB SITES

The Baby Net
Web site: www.thebabynet.com
If you are about to have your first child or already have several, this site is the perfect place to share your knowledge and learn from others. Find furniture manufacturers and answers to your questions, or just join a lively chat with other parents who know exactly what you are going through.

Family.com
Web site: www.family.com
If it pertains to the family, this site has it. Topics covered include choosing the right color scheme for your child's nursery and dealing with a demanding child. Also has information on family pets, travel, shopping, and health.

KidsSafe

Web site: www.kidssafe.com

This Web site concentrates on keeping your child safe. Contains information on childproofing your home, household poisons and local poison-control centers, product recalls, and more.

Parent Zone

Web site: www.parentzone.com

A good resource for parents with children in all stages of development, this site addresses many topics, including a section on baby-proofing your entire house. It even contains a list of baby names if you're looking for some suggestions.

MANUFACTURERS

FURNITURE

Arm's Reach Concepts, Inc.

5699 Kanan Road, Suite 330

Agoura Hills, CA 91301-3358

Phone: 800/954-9353

Web site: www.armsreach.com

Arm's Reach Concepts, Inc., captured a unique idea by manufacturing a co-sleeper. Half bed–half crib, this device sits next to the parents' bed allowing them access to their baby without the dangers of sleeping in the same bed. To check out designs and styles, visit their Web site, or contact them through the information given above to find a local dealer.

The Chair Company

Phone: 800/582-7367

Fax: 336/622-5850

Web site: www.thechaircompany.com

The Chair Company manufactures gliding rockers in eight different collections, and you are free to choose the fabric and finish you want. Great for putting that newborn baby to sleep. Visit their Web site to see samples, or contact the numbers above to find a dealer near you.

Maine Cottage Furniture

PO Box 935

Yarmouth, ME 04096

Phone: 207/846-1430

Fax: 207/846-0602

Web site: www.mainecottage.com

Maine Cottage Furniture offers a colorful alternative to everyday furniture lines. Choose the piece you are looking for from their extensive line of furniture, and then customize it with one of their 40 current colors to match your decor. Check out their Web site for samples, or call to receive a free brochure. For $10, you can even purchase a colorbook featuring 102 pages of full-color photographs and 40 true-to-color paint chips.

Nursery Maid

Phone: 800/443-8773

Web site: www.nurserymaid.com

Nursery Maid manufacturers furniture for day-care centers, churches, etc. A great place to find storage products for children's rooms, including colorful storage

cubbies like those used in day-care settings. Just visit their Web site to view the products they have available, or call the number above.

Patch Kraft
Phone: 800/866-BABY (2229)
Web site: www.patchkraft.com
Patch Kraft manufacturers bedding for both cribs and twin/full beds. Visit their Web site to see available selections or call for a free catalog.

Stanley Furniture Company
Phone: 540/627-2000
Web site: www.stanleyfurniture.com
Select furniture designed to meet the sleep, study, and storage needs of your child's room. Beds are available in twin size. Visit their Web site for a look at their products. By calling the number above, you can also order a brochure for $5.

Vermont Precision Woodworkers
249 Professional Dr.
Morrisville, VT 05661
Phone: 802/888-7974
Fax: 802/888-3668
Web site: www.vtprecision.com
Processed completely by the company, they have seven different styles of bunk beds and 15 styles of beds, as well as children's toy boxes, chairs and tables, all available in any of five different finishes: Natural, White, Cherry, Colonial, and Cinnamon. See their Web site for examples or call, write, or fax for a brochure.

WALLS
Imperial Home Decor Group
Phone: 800/539-5399
Web site: www.imp-wall.com
The Imperial Home Decor Group wallcoverings collections includes many borders designed with kids in mind. See samples of their designs on their Web site, or call the number above to locate a dealer near you.

Stencil Ease
PO Box 1127
Old Saybrook, CT 06475
Phone: 800/334-1776
Web site: www.stencilease.com
If you are looking for stencils to decorate a room, visit this Web site. Directions are included for the beginner. For a catalog, send $5 for shipping and handling to the address above or call for more information.

The Warner Company
Phone: 800/685-8822, ext. 24
Web site: www.thewarnerco.com
You'll discover an extensive collection of wallpaper and borders that would appeal not only to small children but teens as well. See samples of their designs on their Web site or call the number above to locate a dealer near you.

FLOORS
DuPont Stainmaster
Phone: 800/438-7668
Web site: www.dupont.com/Stainmaster
If you are carpeting a child's room, you might want to consider a pre-treated carpet for all those spills your child can leave behind. Visit their Web site for information on this product and answers to your questions, or call the number above. Your local dealers can tell you about availability.

Pergo
Phone: 800/337-3746
Web site: www.usa.pergo.com
Pergo can give you the look of natural wood without the hassle involved with cleaning it. Each type comes with wall-to-wall warranty covering wear-through, stains, fading, and water damage. Visit their Web site for more information and to order a brochure, or call the phone number listed above.

WINDOWS

Hunter Douglas Window Fashions Division

Phone: 800/937-7895

Web site: www.hunterdouglas.com

Hunter Douglas window fashions are custom manufactured for your windows giving you a variety of choices in privacy and light control with endless decorating possibilities in fabric, texture, color, and style. Their Break-Thru® Safety Tassel prevents children and pets from becoming injured if caught in the blind cords. Call or visit their Web site for further information.

SPECIAL NEEDS

Let's Learn Educational Toys, Inc.

2402 Avenue J

Brooklyn, NY 11210

Phone: 800/675-0090

Fax: 718/258-7954

Web site: www.letslearntoys.com

Let's Learn Educational Toys are perfect for a child with allergies. They are made of nonallergic and non-toxic materials, which are machine washable and dryer safe. Their full product line includes bright, colorful printed playmats with skid-proof backing in such fun themes as Hopscotch, Climb and Slide (with large die), and even the basic ABCs. Visit their Web site to see the other toys that they manufacture for your allergy sensitive child, or contact them via the information above.

TFH USA

4537 Gibsonia Road

Gibsonia, PA 15044

Phone: 800/467-6222

Web site: www.tfhusa.com

TFH makes a line of toys and products for children and adults with special needs. Their recreational products are specifically designed for the physically handicapped. Check their Web site for an example of their products, or write or call for their catalog.

ACCESSORIES

American Creative Team, Inc.

Phone: 800/747-5689

Web site: www.us-act.com

American Creative Team, Inc., manufactures many educational toys, including wall hangings and floor mats. A great way to accent your child's room. To view their product line, visit their Web site, or call the number above for more information.

Flip-N-Flush

c/o PU Digital, Inc.

PO Box 390361

Mountain View, CA 94043

Phone: 408/244-0270

Web site: www.flipnflush.com

Flip-N-Flush manufactures a permanently attachable toilet seat that is just the right size for your child. Instead of having to install and remove the potty seat every time, the child can just flip down this attached seat. It can be flipped back out of the way afterward. Available in four colors: red, green, blue, and white. Visit their Web site for more information and to order, or call.

Parent Units

c/o TV Guard Inc.

15 Chestnut Way

Manalapan, NJ 07726

Phone: 732/446-7181

Fax: 732/792-0035

Web site: www.parentunits.com

This manufacturer specializes in safety products for the home to keep your roving toddler safe. Among the products they manufacture are a furniture-fastening system to stop large furniture from toppling over on a child, and a window stop designed to prevent windows from being pushed open too far, endangering a child. Visit their Web site, or call for more information.

CREDITS

Photographers and Designers

Cover: *Photography:* Mark Samu; *Design:* Diane Boyer, ASID, Diane Boyer Interiors, a div. of Bill Behrle Associates, assisted by Therese Rooney. **p. 1** *Photography:* Lilo Raymond/Baby Fortunoff. **p. 2** *Photography:* Nancy Hill; *Design:* Judith Cohen. **p. 6** *Photography:* Hal Lott. **p. 8** *Photography:* Tony Giammarino; *Design:* Patti Ryan. **p. 10** *Photography:* Lilo Raymond/Baby Fortunoff. **pp. 12–15** *Photography:* Mark Samu; *Design:* EJR Architects; *Painting:* Inpaint Workshops and Studio. **p. 16** *Photography:* Mark Samu; *Design:* LeeNajman Design. **p. 17** *Photography:* Hal Lott. **p. 19** *Photography:* Bruce McCandless; *Design:* Rina Capodieci and Jules Vecchione, Higher Limit Design. **pp. 20–22** *Photography:* Bruce McCandless. **p. 23** *Photography:* Hal Lott. **p. 24** *Photography:* Beth Singer; *Design:* Leslie Benser Luciani for the Junior League of Detroit Showhouse. **p. 26** *Photography:* Janet Henderson. **pp.** 26–27 *Photography:* Mark Lohman; *Design:* Lynn Pries. **p. 27** *Photography, top and bottom:* Jessie Walker. **p. 28:** *Photography:* Julie Maris/Semel. **pp. 31–32** *Photography:* Jessie Walker. **p. 33** *Photography:* Tony Giammarino; Patti Ryan. **p. 35** *Photography:* Beth Singer; *Design:* Leslie Benser Luciani for the Junior League of Detroit Showhouse. **p. 36** *Photography:* Courtesy of Maine Cottage Furniture, Inc. **p. 38** *Photography:* Lilo Raymond. **p. 40** *Photography, left:* Mark Samu; *Design:* EJR Architects. *Photography, above right:* Nancy Hill; Design. Stirling Design Associates. *Photography, below right:* Roy Inman; Stylist. Susan Andrews. **p. 41** *Photography:* Phillip Ennis; *Design:* Susann Kelly. **p. 42** *Photography, above left and right; Design:* Rene Hennnessy. *Photography, below:* Mark Lohman. **p. 43** *Photography, left:* Courtesy of Maine Cottage Furniture, Inc. *Photography, above right and below right:* Mark Samu; *Design:* EJR Architects; *Painting:* Inpaint Workshops and Studio. **p. 44** *Photography, left:* John Schwartz. *Photography, right:* Melabee M Miller; *Design:* Suzanne Curtis, Suzanne Curtis Interior Design. **p. 45** *Photography:* Charlie Mayer; *Design:* Michelle Rohrer, Michelle's Interiors. **p. 46** *Photography:* Courtesy of Maine Cottage Furniture, Inc. **pp. 47–48** *Photography:* davidduncanlivingston.com. **p. 50** *Photography, left:* davidduncanlivingston.com. *Photography, right:* Mark Lohman; *Design:* Janet Lohman. **p. 51** *Photography:* Mark Lohman; *Design:* Debbie Jones. **p. 52** *Photography:* Mark Lohman; *Design:* Kathryne Dahlman, Kathryne Designs. **p. 53** *Photography, left:* Janet Henderson. *Photography, right:* Hal Lott. **p. 54** *Photography:* Mark Lohman; *Design:* Kitty Bartholomew; *Design, right:* Janet Lohman. **p. 55** *Photography:* Jessie Walker. **pp. 57–58** *Photography:* Mark Lohman; *Design:* Janet Lohman. **p. 59** *Photography, left:* Hal Lott. *Photography, above right:* Holly Stickley. *Photography, below right:* Courtesy of Motif Designs. **p. 60** *Photography:* Courtesy of Motif Designs. **p. 61** *Photography, left:* Jessie Walker. *Photography, right:* Tony Giammarino; *Design:* Molster & Valentine Interiors **p. 63** *Photography:* Jessie Walker. **p. 64** *Photography, left:* Courtesy of Motif Designs. *Photography, right:* Jessie Walker. **p. 65** *Photography:* Mark Lohman; *Design:* Ge Ge Pender. **p. 66** *Photography, above:* Mark Lohman; *Design:* Janet Lohman. *Photography, below left:* Roy Inman; *Stylist:* Susan Andrews. *Photography, below right:* Mark Lohman; *Design:* Kathryne Dahlman, Kathryne Designs. **p. 67** *Photography, below left:* Bruce McCandless; *Design:* Rina Capodieci and Jules Vecchione, Higher Limit Design. *Photography, above right:* Tony Giammarino; *Design:* Molster & Valentine Interiors. **p. 68** *Photography, left:* Rich Vogel; *Design:* Tracey Stephens Design. *Photography, above right:* Janet

Henderson. *Photography, below right:* Jessie Walker. **p. 69** *Photography:* Mark Lohman; *Design:* Pam Volante. **p. 70** *Photography, left:* davidduncanlingston.com. *Photography, right:* Mark Samu; *Design:* EJR Architects; *Painting:* Inpaint Workshops and Studio. **p. 71** *Photography:* Nancy Hill; *Design:* Judith Cohen. **p. 73** *Photography:* Mark Lohman; *Design:* Lynn Pries. **p. 74** *Photography:* Courtesy of Motif Designs. **pp. 76–77** *Photography:* Mark Samu, Courtesy of Hearst Special Publications. **p. 79** *Photography:* Jessie Walker. **p. 80** *Photography, left:* Courtesy of Motif Designs. *Photography, right:* Jessie Walker. **p. 81** Janet Henderson. **p. 82** *Photography:* Peter Tata. **p. 83** *Photography:* Lilo Raymond. **p. 84** *Photography, left:* Hal Lott. *Photography, right:* Janet Henderson. **p. 85** *Photography:* Nancy Hill; *Design:* Karyne Johnson, Panache Interiors **p. 86** *Photography:* Beth Singer. **p. 88** *Photography, left:* Janet Henderson. *Photography, right:* davidduncanlivingston.com. **p. 89** *Photography:* Don Wong. **p. 90** *Photography:* Brian Vanden Brink; *Design:* Theodore & Theodore Architects. **p. 92** *Photography:* Mark Lohman; *Design:* Janet Lohman. **p. 93** *Photography:* Bruce McCandless. **p. 94** *Photo-*

graphy: Jessie Walker. **p. 95** *Photography, left:* Nancy Hill. *Photography, right:* Hal Lott. **p. 96** *Photography, above:* Lilo Raymond. *Photography, below left:* Bruce McCandless. *Photography, below right:* davidduncanlivingston.com. **p. 97** *Photography:* Mark Lohman. **p. 98** *Photography, left:* Julie Maris/Semel. *Photography, right:* Bruce McCandless. **p. 99** *Photography:* Lilo Raymond. **p. 100** *Photography:* Melabee M Miller; *Design:* Suzanne Curtis, Suzanne Curtis Interior Design. **pp. 102–105** *Photography:* George Ross. **p. 106** *Photography:* Mark Lohman; *Design:* Kathryne Dahlman, Kathryne Designs. **pp. 108–109** *Photography:* Brian Vanden Brink; *Design:* Mary Douglas Drysdale. **p. 110** *Photography:* Mark Samu; *Design:* LeeNajman Design. **p. 111** *Photography:* Nancy Hill; *Design:* Judith Driscoll. **p. 112** *Photography, left:* Nancy Hill; *Design:* Judith Driscoll. *Photography, right:* Janet Henderson. **p. 113** *Photography, below left:* Courtesy of Maine Cottage Furniture, Inc. *Photography, above right:* Melabee M Miller; *Design.* Suzanne Curtis, Suzanne Curtis Interior Design. **p. 114** *Photography:* Roy Inman; *Stylist:* Susan Andrews. **p. 116** *Photography:* Mark Lohman. **p. 117** *Photography:* Jessie Walker.

p. 120–121 *Photography:* Charlie Mayer; *Design:* Michelle Rohrer, Michelle's Interiors. **p. 122** *Photography, left:* Charlie Mayer; *Design:* Michelle Rohrer, Michelle's Interiors. *Photography, right:* Bruce McCandless. **pp. 124–125** *Photography:* Mark Lohman. **p. 126** *Photography:* Bruce McCandless. **pp. 128–129** *Photography:* Mark Samu; *Design:* Diane Boyer, ASID, Diane Boyer Interiors, a div. of Bill Behrle Associates, assisted by Therese Rooney. **p. 130** *Photography:* Tony Giammarino. **p. 131** *Photography:* Mark Samu; *Design:* Diane Boyer, ASID, Diane Boyer Interiors, a div. of Bill Behrle Associates, assisted by Therese Rooney. **p. 132** *Photography:* Lilo Raymond. **p. 133** *Photography:* Mark Lohman; *Design:* Kitty Batholomew. **pp. 135–137** *Photography:* George Ross. **p. 138** *Photography:* Jennifer Deane. **p. 140** *Photography:* Mark Lohman. **p. 141** *Photography:* Janet Henderson. **p. 142** *Photography:* davidduncanlivingston.com. **p. 143** *Photography:* Tony Giammarino ; *Design:* Patti Ryan. **pp. 144–146** *Photography:* Kari Haavisto; *Design:* Suzanne Felber, Memory Merchandising. **p. 147** *Photography:* Hal Lott. **p. 148** *Photography:* Mark Samu. **p. 150** *Photography:* Melabee M Miller;

Design: Susan Rosenthal. **p. 151** *Photography:* Mark Samu. **p. 152** *Photography:* Brian Vanden Brink; *Design:* Atlantic Kitchens. **p. 159:** *Photography:* John Schwartz. **p. 160:** *Photography:* Mark Samu; *Design:* Diane Boyer, ASID. **p. 162:** *Photography:* Tony Giammarino, *Design:* Patti Ryan. **p. 163:** George Ross. **p. 164:** *Photography:* davidduncanlivinston.com. **p. 169:** *Photography:* Bruce McCandless. **p. 170:** *Photography:* Mark Lohman. **p. 175:** *Photography:* Melabee M Miller.

Additional Credits
On the cover: *Fabrics:* Waverly, Maharam, Bergamo, Jab, and Houle. *Bed and Night Stands:* Julia Gray. *Custom Desk Unit:* The Hammer & Nail, Inc. *Love Seat:* William Allan. *Rabbit Lamps:* McEnroe. *Window-Treatment Fabricator:* Alicia Comforts. *Custom Bedding Fabricator:* L & G Decorator Workroom, Inc.

Bedroom pictured on pages 128–129, 131: *Fabrics:* Bloomcraft, Intex, Robert Allen, and Houle. *Bed and Chaise Longue:* Swaim. *Bedding:* Swaim. *Desk and Chair:* HBF. *Window-Treatment Fabricator:* L & G Decorator Workroom, Inc. *Custom Painting:* Holsten Interior Artisans.

INDEX

Have a home decorating, improvement, or gardening project? Look for these and other fine **Creative Homeowner books** wherever books are sold. . .

Projects to personalize your rooms with paint and paper. 300 color photos. 176 pp.; 9"×10"
BOOK #: 279723

Learn how to make the most of color. More than 150 color photos. 176 pp.; 9"×10"
BOOK #: 287264

How to create kitchen style like a pro. Over 150 color photographs. 176 pp.; 9"×10"
BOOK #: 279935

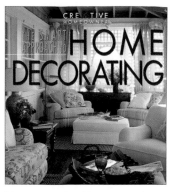

How to work with space, color, pattern, texture. Over 300 photos. 256 pp.; 9"×10"
BOOK #: 279667

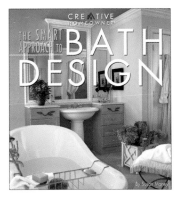

All you need to know about designing a bath. Over 150 color photos. 176 pp., 9"×10"
BOOK # 279225

Design advice and industry tips for choosing window treatments. Over 225 illustrations. 176 pp., 9"×10"
BOOK # 279431

Master stenciling, sponging, glazing, marbling, and more. Over 300 illustration. 272 pp., 9"×10"
BOOK #: 279550

Interior designer Lyn Peterson's easy-to-live-with decorating ideas. Over 350 photos. 304 pp., 9"×10"
BOOK #: 279382

Complete houseplant guide. 200 readily available plants; more than 400 photos. 192 pp.; 9"×10"
BOOK #: 275243

Create more beautiful, healthier, lower-maintenance lawns. Over 300 illustrations. 160 pp.; 9"×10"
BOOK #: 274359

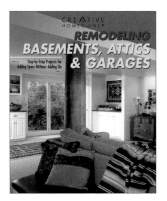

How to convert unused space into useful living area. 570 illustrations. 192 pp.; $8^{1}/_{2}$"×$10^{7}/_{8}$"
BOOK #: 277680

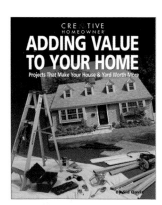

Filled with DIY projects to repair, upgrade, and add value. 500 illustrations. 176 pp.; $8^{1}/_{2}$"×$10^{7}/_{8}$"
BOOK #: 277006